ADVANCED EXCEL 365

Including ChatGPT Tips

ADVANCED EXCEL 365

Including ChatGPT Tips

RITU ARORA

MERCURY LEARNING AND INFORMATION
Boston, Massachusetts

Publisher: David Pallai
MERCURY LEARNING AND INFORMATION
121 High Street, 3rd Floor
Boston, MA 02110
info@merclearning.com
www.merclearning.com
800-232-0223

R. Arora. *Advanced Excel 365:Including ChatGPT Tips.*
ISBN: 978-1-50152-251-2

Library of Congress Control Number: 2024939128

242526321   This book is printed on acid-free paper in the United States of America.

To my beloved father, Ramesh Dhingra,
a guiding light in my Excel journey

CONTENTS

*P*REFACE

This book will explore the powerful trio of Excel^{TM}, Visual Basic for Applications (VBA)^{TM}, and ChatGPT. These tools combine the strength of data analysis, automation, and conversational AI to empower you in the realm of information processing and decision-making.

Throughout these pages, you will be provided with practical knowledge, hands-on examples, and step-by-step instructions to master Excel's data manipulation capabilities, unlock the potential of VBA for automation and customization, and study ChatGPT for natural language interactions.

Whether you are a beginner seeking to understand the basics, or an experienced user looking to enhance your skills, this book will serve as your roadmap to excel in these domains. It will guide you through the fundamentals of Excel, introduce you to the world of VBA programming, and show you how to integrate ChatGPT into your applications for dynamic and intelligent conversations.

This book will explore the endless possibilities of Excel, VBA, and ChatGPT. Here is a brief look at the various chapters:

Chapter 1: Overview of Excel 2021

Discover the new interface, components, and features of Excel 2021, including online file sharing, customizing the ribbon, and leveraging flash fills and instant data analysis for efficient data entry.

Chapter 2: Cell References and Range

Learn about several types of cell references and named ranges for easier referencing. Practice these concepts with hands-on exercises.

Chapter 3: Working with Formulas and Functions

Master Excel's formulas and functions, including IF variations, lookup functions, and dynamic VLOOKUP. Reinforce your understanding through practical exercises.

Chapter 4: Data Validation

Set data validation rules to ensure data accuracy. Explore custom validation techniques through practical exercises.

Chapter 5: Protection

Secure your Excel files by protecting worksheets, workbooks, and specific parts with passwords.

Chapter 6: Sorting a Database

Organize data efficiently using simple, multilevel, and customized sorting methods.

Chapter 7: Filtering a Database

Filter data with Auto Filter and advanced filtering techniques to extract relevant information.

Chapter 8: Subtotals and Data Consolidation

Summarize and analyze data using the Subtotal feature and consolidate data from multiple sources.

Chapter 9: Pivot Tables

Create and format PivotTables for versatile data analysis, including advanced features like grouping items and generating graphs.

Chapter 10: Conditional Formatting

Apply cell value-based and formula-based formatting, including advanced techniques with multiple conditions.

Chapter 11: What-if-Analysis

Use What-if-Analysis tools, like Goal Seek and data tables, to project figures and create scenarios.

Chapter 12: Working with Multiple Worksheets, Workbooks, and Applications

Link different worksheets and software, merge workbooks, and track changes for collaborative work.

Chapter 13: Working with Charts

Create and customize charts using Chart Tools, templates, and sparklines to enhance data visualization.

Chapter 14: Creating and Recording Macros in VBA

Automate tasks by creating and recording macros, including relative reference macros.

Chapter 15: Assigning Buttons to Macros

Enhance user interaction by creating and customizing menus and buttons for macros.

Chapter 16: Functions and Subroutines in VBA

Understand and write functions and subroutines in VBA, including branching techniques.

Chapter 17: Conditional Statements in VBA

Use Select Case and If...End If statements to control program flow efficiently.

Chapter 18: Variables and Data Types in VBA

Declare variables and constants, understand data types, and use message boxes and input boxes.

Chapter 19: Looping Structures in VBA

Implement loops, like Do...Loop and For...Next, to repeat actions in VBA code.

Chapter 20: Arrays and Collections in VBA

Work with arrays and collections to store and manage multiple values effectively.

Chapter 21: Debugging and Error Handling in VBA

Manage errors and debug VBA code to resolve issues efficiently.

Chapter 22: User Forms and User Input in VBA

Design interactive user forms with controls like buttons and text boxes for enhanced user input.

Chapter 23: Advanced VBA Techniques and Best Practices

Explore advanced programming techniques and follow best practices for efficient VBA coding.

Chapter 24: Building Custom Add-ins with VBA

Create custom Add-ins to extend Excel's functionality and protect them with passwords.

Chapter 25: ChatGPT with Excel

Integrate ChatGPT with Excel for enhanced tasks, content generation, and data analysis while maintaining data privacy and security.

Color images are available for downloading by writing to the publisher at info@merclearning.com.

By the end of this book, you will have the knowledge and confidence to leverage the combined power of Excel, VBA, and ChatGPT to streamline your workflows, automate repetitive tasks, and engage in intelligent, data-driven conversations.

ACKNOWLEDGMENTS

I would like to extend my heartfelt gratitude and acknowledgements to the following individuals, whose unwavering support and love have been a constant source of inspiration and encouragement throughout the creation of this book:

To my supportive husband, Mr. Harsh Arora, whose unwavering belief in my abilities and unconditional love have been my anchor. Your encouragement and understanding during the writing process have been invaluable, and I am truly blessed to have you by my side.

To my dear mother, Mrs. Asha Dhingra, and my in-laws, Mrs. Shakun Arora and Mr. K. K. Arora, for their endless encouragement, love, and sacrifices. Their unwavering belief in my dreams and their constant presence in my life was a driving force behind the completion of this book.

To my cherished children, Vansh Arora and Mannat Arora, whose patience and understanding during this time have been remarkable. Your unwavering support and bright smiles have been a constant source of motivation, reminding me of the importance of balance and family throughout this endeavor.

To my sisters, Mrs. Sudha Khurana and Mrs. Namrata Lal, extended family, and friends, for their continual support, words of encouragement, and belief in my abilities. Your unwavering faith in me has given me the strength to overcome challenges and pursue my passion.

To the readers of this book, who have entrusted me with their time and curiosity. It is my sincere hope that the knowledge and insights shared within these pages will inspire and empower you on your own Excel journey.

I am immensely grateful for the contributions and support of each and every one of you. Thank you for being an integral part of this journey.

ABOUT THE AUTHOR

Ritu Arora is a highly skilled and experienced Microsoft Certified Trainer, specializing in Power BI, Excel, PowerPoint, G Suite, and ChatGPT. With over 20 years of corporate training experience, including international assignments, Ritu has successfully trained over 70,000 individuals at companies like DDFS, EY, RateGain, LG, IIMs, SMBC, Ericsson, HCL, Tata Advanced Systems, BPCL, Nestle, Citibank, Adidas, and Hero Honda. Her expertise, excellent communication skills, and ability to tailor training programs to specific needs have made her a sought-after corporate trainer.

1

OVERVIEW OF EXCEL 2021

INTRODUCTION

Excel 2021 is a subscription-based version of Microsoft Excel that is part of the Microsoft 365 suite of productivity tools. It is a cloud-based version of Excel that provides users with access to the latest features and updates. Here is an overview of some of the key features of Excel 2021:

- *Collaborative Editing:* Excel 2021 allows multiple users to edit a spreadsheet simultaneously, making it easier for teams to work together on projects.
- *Cloud Storage:* Excel 2021 files are stored in the cloud, which means they can be accessed from anywhere with an internet connection.
- *Power Query:* Excel 2021 includes Power Query, a tool that allows users to connect to and import data from a variety of sources.
- *Dynamic Arrays:* With dynamic arrays, users can perform calculations on a range of values and return multiple results in a single cell.
- *Artificial Intelligence:* Excel 2021 includes AI-powered features that can analyze data and provide insights. This includes tools such as the Ideas feature, which suggests charts, graphs, and other visualizations.
- *New Chart Types:* Excel 2021 includes new chart types, such as the funnel chart and the map chart, which allow users to display data in new and interesting ways.
- *Improved Data Analysis:* Excel 2021 includes new data analysis tools, such as the Data Types feature, which allow users to convert raw data into structured data that can be used in calculations and analysis.

MS Excel is a spreadsheet software, which is a tool used to record data, support plotting, and analyze the entered data. This is a powerful tool with numerous features that can be used to track a budget, create a record of sales or invoices or maintain a training log. You can store the details of your products or service inquiries, or explore its other business applications.

As in the previous version, this version has a set of menus at the top of the window known as the Ribbon. All the Excel commands are present on the menu. An Excel document is known as a Workbook, and each Workbook is divided into a set of rows and columns. An intersection of this tabular structure is known as a Cell. Data is entered into cells. In fact, all operations performed in the spreadsheet are applied to the cells. MS Excel has a set of tools by which users can format data, perform analysis, and create charts.

STRUCTURE

This chapter will cover the following topics:

- Components of the Excel window
- Backstage view
- Saving and sharing files online
- Interacting with Excel
- Working with default settings
- Formatting a table
  - Paste Special preview
  - Flash fills
- Quick Data analysis
- Data Mining
- TAT saving technique

OBJECTIVES

After studying this chapter, the reader should be able to understand the new layout of MS Excel, figure out how to change the default settings, understand the tool in general, and identify the different types of references, as well as the Named Ranges.

COMPONENTS OF THE EXCEL WINDOW

FIGURE 1.1 Excel Welcome Window

When you open Excel by clicking its shortcut, a unique landing page known as the Welcome page appears. This welcome page offers various sample spreadsheets, such as movie lists, personal budgeting, trend, analysis, and more. Most importantly, it offers the Blank worksheet option, with which users can open a blank spreadsheet and enter the data according to their requirements. The Welcome Window of Excel is shown in *Figure 1.1*.

This window also has a text field that allows the user to search for online templates. This can be used to synchronize the user's Excel interface with the online MS office templates library.

When you double-click the Blank window option, a blank spreadsheet opens, as shown in *Figure 1.2*.

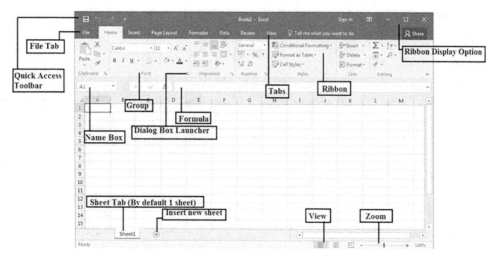

FIGURE 1.2 Various Components of an Excel 2016 Window

BACKSTAGE VIEW

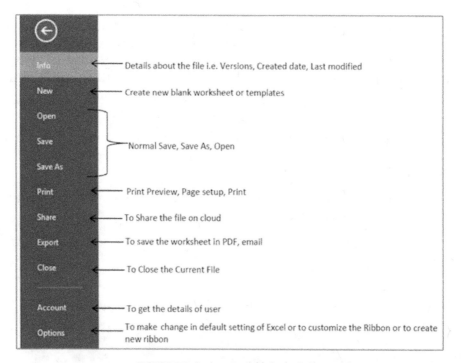

FIGURE 1.3 Options Available in the Backstage View

From the Backstage view, you can manage your documents and the data related to them. Here, you can create, send, and inspect documents for hidden metadata or personal information. The File tab replaces the MS Office button and the File menu used in the earlier releases of MS Office. *Figure 1.3* features the various options available in the Backstage view:

Below are the various options available in the Backstage view:

- *Quick Access Toolbar:* This toolbar is present at the top left corner of the window. It contains commands for saving the current workbook and undoing and redoing actions. This toolbar can be customized by adding buttons for frequently used commands. It is movable and can be moved underneath the Ribbon.
- *Ribbon:* The Ribbon is organized into various tabs, with each ribbon tab activating a ribbon. Each tab is divided into a set of commands known as groups, which contain commands and options that relate to the group name.
- *Gallery:* A Gallery may be displayed within a Ribbon, but more often, it is a drop-down group of commands or functions. The Gallery uses icons or other graphics to show the result of commands rather than the commands themselves. *Figure 1.4* shows the gallery options.

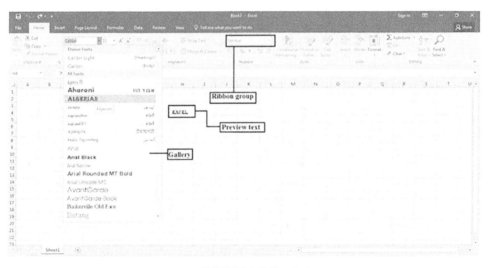

FIGURE 1.4 Gallery Options

SAVING AND SHARING FILES ONLINE

Even if you do not have MS Office 365 or any of its versions, you can still access and view the essentials for free online. Refer to *Figure 1.5.*

FIGURE 1.5 Share Option in the Backstage View

INTERACTING WITH EXCEL

There are various ways by which any user can interact with the Excel worksheet. These are typing or using the mouse to choose a command, make selections, click buttons, and other do other actions.

- *Using the Ribbon:* The Ribbon is a main container for menus and tools. When you choose a Ribbon tab, it displays Ribbon groups, which contains tools (buttons and lists). Some of these tools expand to display simple lists and the gallery, as shown in *Figure 1.3.*
- *Using Galleries:* The Gallery is an interactive list of options which display the option under the click command. For example, the font gallery shows a list of fonts available. Some galleries use live preview, so that when you move the pointer over the options on a gallery, each option is previewed. For example, if you select text in the worksheet and display

the font gallery, moving the pointer over each font in the gallery causes the selected text on the screen to display in that font. Refer to *Figure 1.4.*

■ *Using Tools:* When you keep your mouse pointer over any tool, a small description about the tool appears, which is called a super tooltip. It provides a small description about the tool so you can understand what exactly the tool can do.

TIP *Press Alt+F4 to see the shortcuts related to the option inside the ribbon.*

WORKING WITH DEFAULT SETTINGS

Excel allows you to customize various aspects, behaviors, and methods by which you can interact with it. You can change the default settings of Excel, including font, number of iterations, file locations, and the file which opens on starting Excel. To select the dialog box of options, you need to click the File Tab button and then select Options, as shown in *Figure 1.6:*

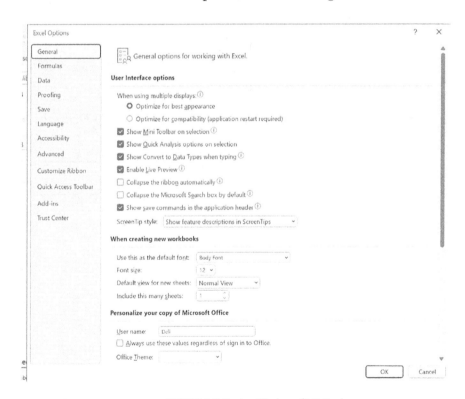

FIGURE 1.6 Option Window of MS Excel

The various options are as follows:

- *Personalize Options:* You can change the workbook settings by using the Personalize Options tool to change the type and size of the font, the number of worksheets in the workbook, and to activate the Developer tab, which is used for Macros.
- *Save Option:* This option allows you to change the default file location, file format, and Auto Recover settings of the file.
- *Customize the Ribbon:* In Excel, you can create custom tabs and groups, and rename or change the order of the built-in tabs and groups. In the Customize the Ribbon list, the custom tabs and groups have "custom" after the name, but the word "custom" does not appear in the ribbon.
- *Adding a Custom Tab and a Custom Group:* Here we have a set of steps by which we can add a custom tab and custom group in the ribbon. Command can be added only in the custom groups.

To add a custom tab, follow these steps:

1. Click the File tab.

2. Click the Options button under Help.

3. Click Customize Ribbon.

4. Click New Tab.

5. To see and save your customizations, click OK. Refer to *Figure 1.7.*

FIGURE 1.7 Steps to Customize a Custom Tab and a Custom Group

FORMATTING OF TABLES

Excel provides various predefined table styles that we can use to format a table quickly. It is a format which is provided by Excel, so we do not have to change the style of or font used in the table.

You can format the table by using the following steps:

1. Select the range.

2. Select Home on Ribbon.

3. Select the Style Group.

4. Select the Format Table. This option opens the various format styles in the form of a drop-down list. By clicking on any style, you can apply it to your data.

Paste Special Preview

Excel offers you the Paste with Live Preview feature, which enables you to save time when reusing content. This option helps you see the preview of various available paste options, such as keeping source column widths, use of borders, and whether or not to keep source formatting. The live preview enables you to see how your pasted content will look before you paste it into the worksheet. When you move your pointer over Paste Options to preview results, you will see a menu containing items that change contextually to best fit the content you are reusing. ScreenTips provide additional information to help you to make the right decision.

Flash Fill

This is an exciting new feature which promises to save time. Consider an example: if you write first name in Column A and last name in Column B, and want to concatenate both names in column C, Excel uses the Flash Fill feature to auto-fill the entire column, as shown in *Figure 1.8 (a)*. As another example, suppose we have email addresses with full names in Column A. You can start entering the first names in a new column, and Excel will auto-fill the entire column, as shown in *Figure 1.8 (b)*.

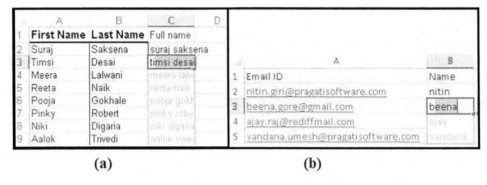

FIGURE 1.8 Flash Fill

QUICK DATA ANALYSIS

Quick analysis is a new tool added to Excel which enables single click access to data analysis features such as formulas, conditional formatting, spark lines, tables, charts, and Pivot Tables. You just need to select some data and right click and see various Quick Analysis options.

In this example, there is data arranged in department-wise salary, but it needs to be presented in a proper format. You need to do a quick analysis. Refer to *Figure 1.9*:

FIGURE 1.9 The Quick Data Analysis Tool

DATA MINING

Advanced Excel has several features that can be used for data mining, which is the process of discovering patterns and insights from large datasets. Here are some of the key data mining features in Excel:

- *PivotTables*: PivotTables allow you to summarize and analyze large datasets quickly and easily. You can use PivotTables to create interactive reports, identify trends, and discover patterns in your data. *Figure 1.10* shows the PivotTables icon:

PivotTable

FIGURE 1.10 PivotTables

- *Conditional Formatting*: Conditional Formatting allows you to highlight specific data based on certain criteria. This can be useful for identifying outliers, spotting trends, and identifying patterns in your data. *Figure 1.11* shows the Conditional Formatting icon:

Conditional
Formatting ▾

FIGURE 1.11 Conditional Formatting

- *Data Validation*: Data Validation allows you to set rules for data entry in your spreadsheets. This can help ensure data integrity and accuracy, which is important for effective data mining. *Figure 1.12* shows the icon for data validation:

Data
Validation ▾

FIGURE 1.12 Data Validation

■ *What-if Analysis*: What-if Analysis allows you to explore different scenarios and their potential outcomes. This can be useful for forecasting, risk analysis, and decision-making. *Figure 1.13* shows the icon for What-if Analysis:

FIGURE 1.13 What-if Analysis

■ *Solver*: Solver is an add-in for Excel that allows you to optimize complex models and solve problems. It can be used for optimization problems, linear programming, and more. Refer to *Figure 1.14*:

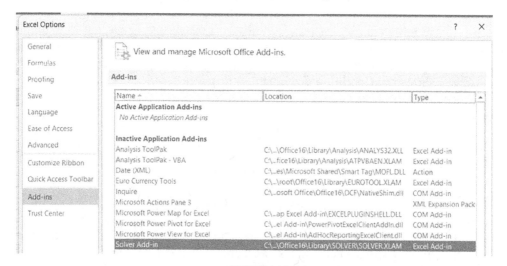

FIGURE 1.14 Solver

■ *Power Query*: Power Query is a data transformation and cleaning tool that can be used to extract, transform, and load data from multiple sources. It can automate data cleaning tasks and prepare data for analysis. Refer to *Figure 1.15*:

Query Options   ×

GLOBAL   Layout

Data Load   ☑ Display the Query Settings pane

Power Query Editor   ☑ Display the Formula Bar

Security   Data Preview

Privacy   ☐ Display preview contents using a monospaced font

Diagnostics   ☑ Show whitespace and newline characters

CURRENT WORKBOOK   Parameters

Data Load   ☐ Always allow parameterization in data source and transformation dialogs

Regional Settings

FIGURE 1.15 Power Query

▪ *Text-to-Columns*: The Text-to-Columns feature allows you to split data in a column into multiple columns based on a delimiter or pattern. This can be useful for cleaning and restructuring your data. *Figure 1.16* shows the icon for Text-to-Column.

Text to
Columns

FIGURE 1.16 Text-to-Columns

By using these data mining features in Excel, you can quickly and easily discover patterns and insights in your data, which can help you make better decisions and achieve your business goals.

TAT SAVING TECHNIQUES

Turnaround time (TAT) reduction techniques in Excel can refer to different methods that aim to speed up the process of working with spreadsheets and reduce the time it takes to perform certain tasks. Here are some techniques that can help improve TAT in Excel:

▪ *Use Keyboard Shortcuts*: Keyboard shortcuts can significantly improve your speed in Excel. For example, you can press *Ctrl+C* to copy and *Ctrl+V* to paste or use the *F2* key to edit a cell.

■ *Use Formulas and Functions*: Excel offers a wide range of built-in formulas and functions that can automate many tasks and save time. For example, some commonly used functions include SUM, AVERAGE, COUNT, IF, and VLOOKUP. The Formulas bar can be seen in *Figure 1.17*:

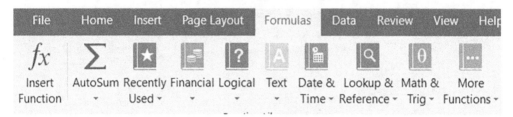

FIGURE 1.17 Formulas in Excel

■ *Use Data Validation*: Data validation is a powerful feature in Excel that allows you to control the type of data that can be entered into a cell. This can help prevent errors and save time by reducing the need to correct mistakes. This option can be seen in the following *Figure 1.18*:

FIGURE 1.18 Data Validation

■ *Use Conditional Formatting*: Conditional formatting allows you to highlight cells that meet certain criteria, making it easier to analyze data and identify trends. This can help save time by reducing the need to manually search for specific values or patterns. This option can be seen in *Figure 1.19*:

FIGURE 1.19 Conditional Formatting

■ *Use Pivot Tables*: Pivot tables are a powerful tool for summarizing and analyzing large datasets. They can help you quickly identify trends and patterns in your data and make it easier to create reports and charts. Refer to *Figure 1.20*:

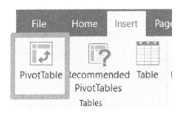

FIGURE 1.20 PivotTable Icon

■ *Use Excel Templates*: Excel templates can save time by providing pre-designed spreadsheets with built-in formulas, formatting, and layouts. This can save time by eliminating the need to create spreadsheets from scratch. Refer to *Figure 1.21*:

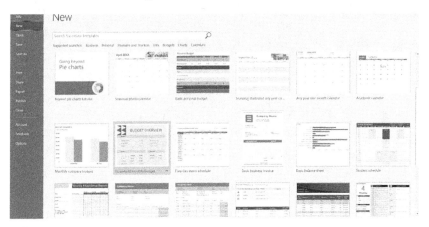

FIGURE 1.21 Excel Templates

■ *Use the Autofill Feature*: The Autofill feature in Excel can save time by automatically filling in a series of values or formulas in a selected range of cells. To use Autofill, select the cell(s) with the desired value or formula, and then drag the fill handle over the range of cells where you want the values or formulas to appear. Refer to *Figure 1.22*:

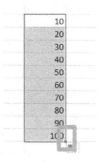

FIGURE 1.22 Autofill Feature

■ *Use Excel's Sorting and Filtering Features*: Excel's sorting and filtering features can save time by quickly organizing and analyzing data. To sort data, select the column you want to sort by and click the Sort A-Z or Sort Z-A button. To filter data, click the Filter button and select the criteria you want to use to filter the data, as shown in *Figure 1.23*:

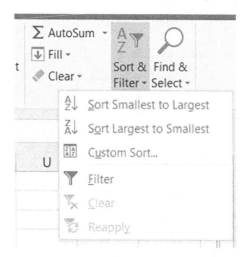

FIGURE 1.23 Sorting and Filtering in Excel

By using these techniques, you can save time and increase your productivity when working with Excel spreadsheets.

CONCLUSION

In summary, Excel 2021 is a powerful tool that offers an array of features for data management, analysis, and collaboration. With its user-friendly interface, customization options, and data analysis capabilities, Excel 2021 empowers users to work efficiently, gain insights, and make informed decisions. It is a versatile tool that enhances productivity and is essential for individuals and businesses dealing with data.

EXERCISES

1. What is the purpose of Excel's conditional formatting feature?

   a. To perform complex calculations

   b. To analyze data trends

   c. To format cells based on specific criteria

   d. To import and export data from other software

2. Which function in Excel allows you to find the highest value in a range of cells?

   a. MAX

   b. SUM

   c. AVERAGE

   d. COUNT

CELL REFERENCES AND RANGE

INTRODUCTION

In this chapter, we will explore the essential concepts of cell references and ranges in spreadsheet applications, enabling us to effectively manipulate and analyze data. By understanding how cell references and ranges work, we can streamline our tasks, perform calculations, and maintain consistency in our spreadsheet work.

STRUCTURE

In this chapter, we will go over the following topics:

- Using different types of references
- Types of cell reference
- Named range

OBJECTIVES

After studying this chapter, the reader will understand the meaning and usage of cell references, as well as the usage of range names. The reader will also be able to identify the various types of cell references.

USING DIFFERENT TYPES OF REFERENCES

When we copy a reference from one cell to another, it gets updated automatically. For example, we have a reference in cell C1 as A1, and we copy the same to D1. This will automatically update itself to B1. Sometimes, we need to keep a part of the used cell references constant. This can be done by using different types of cell references.

TYPES OF CELL REFERENCE

There are three types of cell references:

- Relative Cell Reference
- Absolute Cell Reference
- Mixed Cell Reference

Refer to *Figure 2.1*:

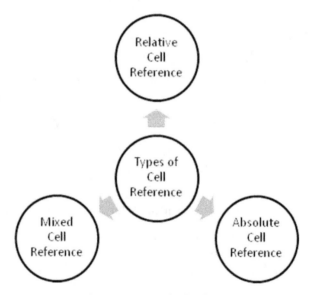

FIGURE 2.1 Types of Cell References

Relative Cell Reference

This is the default cell reference in Excel. In this kind of reference, when you copy and paste a relative cell reference into a cell, the cell is updated automatically according to the change made in the cell from which it has been copied. For example, suppose you want to calculate HRA, which is 50% of the base salary. To do this, you need to type the formula =*H2*50%* in the first cell of the HRA column, as shown in *Figure 2.2*:

	A	B	C	D	E	F	G	H	I
1	Empcode	FirstName	LastName	Dept	Region	Branch	Hiredate	Basic	HRA
2	1	Raja	Raymondekar	Sales	north	Ferozepur	1-Jan-77	15,625.00	=H2*50%
3	2	Suman	Shinde	Sales	east	Cuttack	1-Jan-77	12,500.00	
4	2	Kuldeep	Sharma	Admin	south	Hydrabad	1-Mar-99	5,000.00	
5	3	Beena	Mavadia	Mktg	north	Delhi	24-Nov-70	8,750.00	

FIGURE 2.2 Typing Formula =H2*50% in the First Cell of the HRA Column

To find the HRA for all employees, press the left button of the mouse over the lower right corner of the border of the first cell in the HRA column and drag it down to the last record, as shown in *Figure 2.3:*

	A	B	C	D	E	F	G	H	I
1	Empcode	FirstNam	LastNam	Dept	Region	Branch	Hiredate	Basic	HRA
2	1	Raja	Raymonde	Sales	north	Ferozepur	28126	15625	=H2*50%
3	2	Suman	Shinde	Sales	east	Cuttack	28126	12500	=H3*50%
4	2	Kuldeep	Sharma	Admin	south	Hydrabad	36220	5000	=H4*50%
5	3	Beena	Mavadia	Mktg	north	Delhi	29183	8750	=H5*50%
6	4	Seema	Ranganath	R&D	north	Kanpur	32755	15000	=H6*50%
7	5	Julie	D'Souza	R&D	north	Mathura	32390	8875	=H7*50%

FIGURE 2.3 Dragging the Formula

TIP! *Select the cells to fill and press Ctrl + D to fill the range, or double click on the fill handle.*

Absolute Cell References

If you want to freeze a cell reference, but you do not want a cell reference to change when you copy a formula, you have to use absolute cell reference. To make a cell reference absolute, a dollar sign ($) is placed before the column name and with the row number of the reference.

Suppose you want to find 10% of 1000, 2000, 3000, and 4000, as shown in *Figure 2.4:*

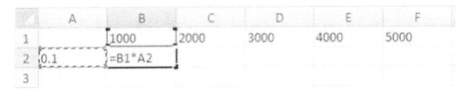

	A	B	C	D	E	F
1		1000	2000	3000	4000	5000
2	0.1	=B1*A2				
3						

FIGURE 2.4 Finding 10% of 1000, 2000, 3000, and 4000

If you write the formula as shown in the previous figure, the formula when copied to the right would change itself to *C1*B2, D1*C2*, and so on. This is not the right calculation, however. We would need to freeze the cell reference A2, such that it remains the same each time we copy the formula. A2 needs to be changed to $A$2 to achieve the required output, as shown in *Figure 2.5*:

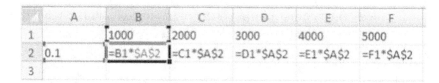

	A	B	C	D	E	F
1		1000	2000	3000	4000	5000
2	0.1	=B1*$A$2	=C1*$A$2	=D1*$A$2	=E1*$A$2	=F1*$A$2
3						

FIGURE 2.5 Write A2 as $A$2

The required result can be seen in *Figure 2.6:*

	A	B	C	D	E	F	G
1		1000	2000	3000	4000	5000	
2	0.1	100	200	300	400	500	
3							

FIGURE 2.6 Result of the Formula Made with Absolute Cell References

TIP! *First, select the cells from B2 to F2, then press Ctrl + R. This will copy the formula from B2 in C2, D2, E2, and F2.*

Mixed Cell Reference

Sometimes you may want to freeze only the row or column in a cell reference. In *Figure 2.7*, we need to calculate *10%, 20%, 30%, 40%,* and *50%* of *1000, 2000, 3000, 4000*, and so on.

	A	B	C	D	E	F
1		1000	2000	3000	4000	5000
2	0.1	=B1*A2				
3	0.2					
4	0.3					
5	0.4					
6	0.5					

FIGURE 2.7 Calculate 10%, 20%, 30%, 40%, and 50% of 1000, 2000, 3000, 4000, and 5000

If you drag the formula toward the right, it changes to *C2∗B3, D2∗C3,* and so on. Once dragged down, it would change to *B3∗A4, B4∗A5,* and so on. These are not the right formulae, however. Refer to *Figure 2.8.*

	A	B	C	D	E	F
1		1000	2000	3000	4000	5000
2	0.1	=B1*A2	=C1*B2	=D1*C2	=E1*D2	=F1*E2
3	0.2	=B2*A3	=C2*B3	=D2*C3	=E2*D3	=F2*E3
4	0.3	=B3*A4	=C3*B4	=D3*C4	=E3*D4	=F3*E4
5	0.4	=B4*A5	=C4*B5	=D4*C5	=E4*D5	=F4*E5
6	0.5	=B5*A6	=C5*B6	=D5*C6	=E5*D6	=F5*E6
7						

FIGURE 2.8 Wrong Formulae in the Referenced Cells

If we observe *Figure 2.8* closely, we can see that we need to freeze the row number of B2 (as it is common for all the formulae toward the right and down) and the column name for A3 (as it is common for all the formulae toward the right and down). When copied, the resultant formulae would be as shown in *Figure 2.9.*

	A	B	C	D	E	F
1		1000	2000	3000	4000	5000
2	0.1	=B$1*$A2	=C$1*$A2	=D$1*$A2	=E$1*$A2	=F$1*$A2
3	0.2	=B$1*$A3	=C$1*$A3	=D$1*$A3	=E$1*$A3	=F$1*$A3
4	0.3	=B$1*$A4	=C$1*$A4	=D$1*$A4	=E$1*$A4	=F$1*$A4
5	0.4	=B$1*$A5	=C$1*$A5	=D$1*$A5	=E$1*$A5	=F$1*$A5
6	0.5	=B$1*$A6	=C$1*$A6	=D$1*$A6	=E$1*$A6	=F$1*$A6
7						

FIGURE 2.9 Resultant Formulae

The answer would be as shown in *Figure 2.10.* References where either the row or the column number is frozen are called Mixed Cell References.

	A	B	C	D	E	F	G
1		1000	2000	3000	4000	5000	
2	0.1	100	200	300	400	500	
3	0.2	200	400	600	800	1000	
4	0.3	300	600	900	1200	1500	
5	0.4	400	800	1200	1600	2000	
6	0.5	500	1000	1500	2000	2500	
7							

FIGURE 2.10 Resultant Values

TIP! *Keep the cursor near the cell reference and press F4 to toggle between the different cell references.*

NAMED RANGE

When you write formulas (also called functions), you need to select a range of cells. It could be time-consuming when the range is large. Excel provides us a way to give a name to the range. For example, we can write *Sum (Basic)* in place of *Sum (H2:H101)*. To do this, we first need to name the range *H2:H10* as Basic. Below are instructions on how to give a name to the range.

Creating a Named Range

To name a range, we may use one of the following procedures:

1. Select the range (for example, *H2:H101*) and type the name (for example, *Sal*) in the name box, as shown in *Figure 2.11*:

	A	B	C	D	E	F	G	H
1	Empcode	First Name	Last Name	Dept	Region	Branch	Hiredate	Salary
2	1	Raja	Raymondekar	Sales	north	Ferozepur	01-Jan-77	21875
3	2	Suman	Shinde	Sales	east	Cuttack	01-Jan-77	17500
4	3	Kuldeep	Sharma	Admin	south	Hydrabad	01-Mar-99	7000
5	4	Beena	Mavadia	Mktg	north	Delhi	24-Nov-79	12250
6	5	Seema	Ranganathan	R&D	north	Kanpur	04-Sep-89	21000
7	6	Julie	D'Souza	R&D	north	Mathura	04-Sep-88	12425
8	7	Deepak	Jain	Personnel	west	Pune	17-Aug-90	13825
9	8	Neena	Mukherjee	R&D	north	Agra	04-Sep-89	12425
10	9	Pankaj	Sutradhar	Sales	north	Ambala	12-Dec-99	14875
11	10	Andre	Fernendes	Mktg	east	Darjeeling	20-Jul-77	15750
12	11	Sujay	Madhrani	Finance	west	Pune	21-Dec-85	14875
13	12	Shilpa	Lele	Admin	north	Jammu	01-Mar-83	21000
14	13	Meera	Lalwani	Finance	east	Calcutta	11-Dec-84	19250
15	14	Sheetal	Desai	Director	south	cochin	12-Dec-84	49000
16	15	K. Sita	Narayanan	Personnel	north	Jammu	13-Dec-84	14875
17	16	Priya	Shirodkar	Personnel	north	Jaipur	14-Dec-84	14875
18	17	Aalok	Trivedi	Admin	east	Cuttack	01-Mar-83	15750
19	18	Aakash	Dixit	Admin	west	Nasik	01-Mar-83	15750
20	19	Parvati	Khanna	Mktg	north	Mathura	13-Aug-86	10500
21	20	Farhan	Sadiq	Mktg	north	Jaipur	05-Jun-99	5950
22	21	Satinder Kaur	Sasan	Mktg	east	Patna	06-Jun-99	7875
23	22	Suchita	Panchal	Mktg	west	Nasik	07-Jun-99	7875

The name box contains "sal" and the formula bar shows "Salary".

FIGURE 2.11 Creating a named range

2. If you want to name the cells with the value in one of the cells, you may select the range along with the name. Click on Create from Selection in the Formulas tab and select one of the options.

3. Click on OK.

4. You may also want to create a named range by clicking on Define name in the Formulas tab.

5. Write the name for the range in the name box. Then click on the Refers to box and select the range you wish to name.

6. Click on OK.

7. Now you can use the given name instead of the range anywhere in the workbook. Refer to *Figure 2.12*:

	B	C	D
	Total Salary	=SUM(sal)	
	Lowest Salary	=MIN(sal)	
	Highest Salary	=MAX(sal)	
	Average of Salary	=AVERAGE(sal)	
	No. of Emp	=COUNT(sal)	

FIGURE 2.12 Use of Named Range Instead of Cell Reference

Editing Named Ranges

Sometimes, it becomes essential to rename or edit the named range. This can be done by taking the following steps:

1. In the Formulas tab, click on Name Manager.

2. A Name Manager dialog box opens, as shown in *Figure 2.13*:

FIGURE 2.13 Name Manager Dialog Box

3. Select the Named Range that you want to edit and click on the Edit button to edit a named range.

4. An Edit Name dialog box appears, as shown in *Figure 2.14*:

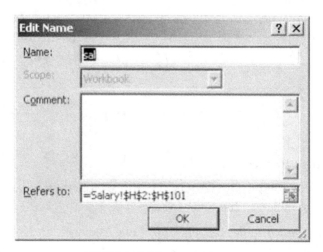

FIGURE 2.14 Edit Name Dialog Box

5. Type a new name or redefine the range name.

Deleting Named Ranges

To delete a range, do the following steps:

1. Select the range from the Name Manager list.

2. Click Delete.

3. The named range will be deleted.

TIP! *Press Ctrl + F3 to open the Name Manager dialog box.*

CONCLUSION

In conclusion, mastering cell references and ranges empowers users to effectively manipulate data and streamline operations in spreadsheet applications, leading to improved efficiency and accuracy in handling large datasets.

EXERCISES

1. Match the correct Relative, Absolute, and Mixed references in *Table 2.1*:

TABLE 2.1 Match the right options

A$1	Relative Reference
$A$1	Absolute Reference
$A1	Mixed Reference

2. In the Excel Training folder, open a file named Advanced Excel Assignment.xlsx. Open "Mixed-Cell sheet" and calculate the percentage sales of each product in different regions in such a way that when you copy the cell formula of east sales and paste in each of the region columns, it automatically calculates sales for the region.

3

WORKING WITH FORMULAS AND FUNCTIONS

INTRODUCTION

In this chapter, we will explore the usage of formulas and functions in Microsoft Excel. Formulas are equations that perform calculations on values, while functions are predefined formulas that simplify complex tasks. We will cover topics such as using formulas in a worksheet, array formulas, using functions, the IF function and its variations, and lookup functions.

STRUCTURE

In this chapter, we will go over the following topics:

- Using formulas in a worksheet
- Using functions
- Lookup functions
- Making V-lookup dynamic
- Index

OBJECTIVES

After studying this chapter, the reader will understand the use of formulas and functions, will be able to identify the different types of functions, and will know how IF and other logical functions work.

USING FORMULAS IN A WORKSHEET

Formulas are the equations that perform calculations on values. A formula starts with an equal sign (=). It contains at least two operands and one operation. For example, the following formula multiplies two by three and adds five to the result.

$$=5+2*3$$

The operand in a formula can be a function, reference, or constant. Operators may be any arithmetic or logical operator.

NOTE   *In Excel, the BODMAS rule is followed to solve a formula when multipleoperators are involved. BODMAS stands for **B**rackets, **O**rder of powers or roots, **D**ivision, **M**ultiplication, **A**ddition, and **S**ubtraction. According to this rule, mathematical expressions with multiple operations should be solved from left to right.*

Array Formula

In *Figure 3.1*, there are five products for which we know the quantity and price. We need to find the Total Sales, which is the result of adding together the quantity and price for all products. In a normal scenario, we would individually calculate the amount for each product and add them to get the answer. To make things simpler, we may also use the Array Formula. Select B8, write *=sum (A2:A6*B2:B6)* and press *Ctrl + Shift + Enter* to fill the formula *{=sum (A1:A3*B1:B3)}* in the selected cell, as shown in *Figure 3.2*. This calculates quantity*price for all the products in cell B8.

NOTE   *Curly brackets ({}) around the formula indicate that it is applied to an array.*

Figure 3.1 features the quantity and price of five products.

	A	B
1	Quantity	Price
2	12	$6.00
3	18	$17.25
4	12	$25.00
5	3	$20.00
6	7	$10.00
7		
8	Tota Sales	

FIGURE 3.1 Quantity and Price of Five Products

Figure 3.2 features the *Quantity*Price* for all products:

B8				f_x	{=SUM(A2:A6*B2:B6)}	
	A	B	C	D	E	F	G
1	Quantity	Price					
2	12	$ 6.00					
3	18	$ 17.25					
4	12	$ 25.00					
5	3	$ 20.00					
6	7	$ 10.00					
7							
8	Total Sale	812.5					
9							
10							

FIGURE 3.2 Quantity*Price for All Products

USING FUNCTIONS

Performing calculations on each value in a range of cells can be complicated and time-consuming. For example, if you have a range consisting of 20 cells, a formula that adds each of these values will be very long. Excel functions simplify complex tasks.

A function is a predefined formula that performs a specific calculation or other action on a number or a text string and returns a value. You may specify the values on which the function performs calculations. The syntax of a function begins with the function name, followed by an opening parenthesis, the arguments for the function separated by commas, and a closing parenthesis.

If the function starts a formula, type an equal sign (=) before the function name. As you create a formula that contains a function, the Formula Palette will assist you, as shown in *Figure 3.3.*

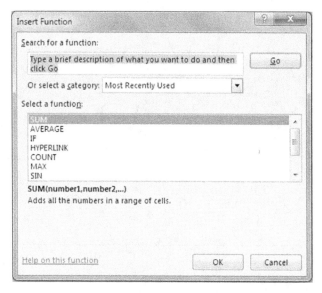

FIGURE 3.3 Inserting a Function

NOTE   *From an empty cell, you may click on the fx symbol near the formula bar to see all the available functions in Excel.*

The syntax of a function is:

```
=Function name (argument1, argument2, ....)
```

Example:

```
=SUM (A10, B5: B10, 50, 37)
```

There is no need to memorize all the functions available and the arguments necessary for each function. You can use sigma sign (d) for sum or click on the drop-down for more functions, like Max, Min, and so on. Excel prompts you for required and optional arguments.

NOTE   *You can use the Alt + = key combination to get the sum function on your worksheet.*

IF Function

In Chapter 2, *Cell References and Range*, we have studied the calculation of income heads such as HRA and DA. The formula we saw was the same for the entire database. According to certain conditions, we need to decide the formula to apply. For example, incentives may be calculated according to the department. This is where conditional functions like "IF" come into the picture.

The IF function can be used for evaluating a condition. Depending on whether the conditions are true or false, the IF function will return the values. The syntax for the IF function is:

```
If(logical_test, [Value_if_true], [Value_if_false])
```

The first argument is the condition that you need the function to evaluate. The second argument is the value to be returned if the condition is true, and the third argument is the value to be returned if the condition is false. The second and third parameters are optional.

EXAMPLE:

Suppose you want to calculate HRA based on the designation of the employees. If the designation is Manager, the HRA is either 1000 or 500. In this case, the function code will be as follows:

```
=if (C2="Manager", 1000, 500)
```

Refer to *Figure 3.4*.

	F2			f_x	=IF(C2="Manager",1000,500)	
	A	B	C	D	E	F	G
1	EMPNO	NAME	DESG	Branch	BASIC	HRA	
2	1	RAJ	OFFICER	Mumbai	5000	500	
3	2	RAJESH	CLERK	Mumbai	3500	500	
4	3	ANAND	MANAGE	Delhi	7000	1000	
5	4	RAJU	CLERK	Delhi	4000	500	
6	5	HEMANT	MANAGE	Mumbai	8000	1000	
7	6	SANTOSF	CLERK	Delhi	3780	500	
8	7	BHAUMIK	OFFICER	Delhi	4200	500	
9	8	MANJIT	OFFICER	Mumbai	5000	500	
10	9	KAMAL	OFFICER	Delhi	3800	500	
11	10	SONU	CLERK	Mumbai	2500	500	
12							

FIGURE 3.4 IF Function

As shown in *Figure 3.4*, the above function calculates HRA as 1000 for Managers and 500 for others.

Nested IF

A nested IF function is used when a second IF function is placed inside the first order function in order to test additional conditions.

The syntax for the Nested IF function is:

```
If (logical_test, [Value_if_true], If (logical_test, [Value_
if_true],[Value_if_false]))
```

EXAMPLE:

You can use nested IF functions to evaluate complex conditions. For example, if the salary is < 5000, the tax is 5%. If the salary is between 5000 and 1000, then it is 10% or it is 15%. Since we have already given the name *sal* to the salary column, we can also use *sal* instead of *h2 =if (sal<5000, salary*.05, if (sal<10000, salary*.10, sal*.15))*. Refer to *Figure 3.5*:

	A	B	C	D	E	F	G	H	I
						I2		fx =IF(H2<5000,H2*0.05,IF(H2<10000,H2*0.1,H2*0.15))	
1	Empcode	FirstNam	LastNam	Dept	Region	Branch	Hiredate	Salary	Tax
2	1	Raja	Raymond	Sales	north	Ferozepur	1-Jan-77	15,625.00	2343.75
3	2	Suman	Shinde	Sales	east	Cuttack	1-Jan-77	12,500.00	1875
4	2	Kuldeep	Sharma	Admin	south	Hydrabad	1-Mar-99	5,000.00	500
5	3	Beena	Mavadia	Mktg	north	Delhi	24-Nov-79	8,750.00	875
6	4	Seema	Ranganath	R&D	north	Kanpur	4-Sep-89	15,000.00	2250
7	5	Julie	D'Souza	R&D	north	Mathura	4-Sep-88	8,875.00	887.5
8	5	Deepak	Jain	Personal	west	Pune	17-Aug-90	9,875.00	987.5

FIGURE 3.5 Using Nested IF Function

Suppose you want to assign letter grades to numbers referenced by the name Average Score, as shown in *Table 3.1*:

TABLE 3.1: Assigning Letter Grades

If Average Score is	Return
Greater than 89	A
From 80 to 89	B
From 70 to 79	C
From 60 to 69	D
Less than 60	F

You can use the following nested IF function:

```
IF (AverageScore>89,"A", IF (AverageScore>79,"B", IF
(AverageScore>69,"C", IF (AverageScore>59,"D","F"))))
```

NOTE *You can nest up to sixty-four levels of IF functions in a single formula.*

IF With AND

In Excel, OR is a logical function which returns false if any one of the arguments returns false.

Syntax:

```
AND (logical1, logical2...)
```

If there is a scenario where we have two conditions whose combined truth value would decide the output of an IF function, we can use AND with IF.

SYNTAX:

```
If (and (Condition1, condition2....), True, False)
```

Example:

If we need to give 10% of a basic salary as incentive to everyone working in the Sales department in the North region, we would use the following formula:

*=IF (AND (Department="sales", Region="north"), 10%*Basic Salary, 0)*

IF With OR

OR is a logical function in Excel, which returns False if any one of the arguments returns false.

Syntax:

```
OR (logical1, logical2...)
```

If there is a scenario where we have two conditions of which any one of the conditions is false, and the IF should return the value in the false argument, we may use OR with IF.

Syntax Using OR With IF

```
If (OR (Condition1, condition2….), True, False)
```

Example:

If the employee is in Sales, Mktg or Hrd, then HRA is 50% of the Basic salary. Otherwise, it is 30% of the Basic salary.

If (or (Department="Mktg", Department ="Sales", Department="Hrd"), Basic salary*.5, Basic salary*.3)

IF With NOT

This is a logical function which is used to negate an argument.

Syntax:

```
NOT (logical)
```

If we have a condition which, when not satisfied, requires us to apply a formula, we may use NOT with IF.

Syntax Using NOT With If

```
If (NOT (Condition), True, False)
```

Example:

If we need to give an incentive to everyone except people working in the Marketing department, we may use the following formula:

IF (NOT (Department="MT"), 10%*salary, 0)

NOTE *There can be maximum of 255 conditions which can be passed to the AND/ORfunction, and we can pass only one condition to NOT.*

We may also use multiple NOT statements inside the IF statement.

Example:

If you need to give an incentive to everyone except people from the sales and admin departments, you may use the following function:

If (and (not (department="Sales"), not (department="admin")), 10%* salary, 0)

LOOKUP FUNCTIONS

Sometimes we need to search for a value in a database using a lookup value. For example, given the Employee ID, how can we look up the incentive value from some other sheet or some other file? In such scenarios, depending on the source database, we may use one of the following lookup functions:

- VLOOKUP (if the database is vertical). Refer to *Figure 3.6:*
- HLOOKUP (if the database is horizontal). Refer to *Figure 3.7:*

	Empcode	First Name	Last Name	Dept	Region	Deptcode	Hiredate	Salary
2								
3	1	Raja	Raymondeka	Sales	north	10	01-Jan-16	125000
4	2	Kuldeep	Sharma	Admin	north	70	01-Mar-17	40000
5	2	Suman	Shinde	Sales	south	10	01-Jan-10	100000
6	3	Beena	Mavadia	Mktg	east	20	24-Nov-12	70000
7	4	Seema	Ranganathan	R&D	north	30	04-Sep-13	120000
8	5	Deepak	Jain	Personal	east	60	17-Aug-04	79000
9	5	Julie	D'Souza	R&D	west	30	04-Sep-06	71000
10	6	Neena	Mukherjee	R&D	north	30	04-Sep-08	71000
11	7	Pankaj	Sutradhar	Sales	north	10	05-Sep-08	85000
12	8	Andre	Fernendes	Mktg	north	20	06-Sep-08	90000
13	9	Sujay	Madhrani	Finance	east	40	07-Sep-08	85000
14	10	Shilpa	Lele	Admin	west	70	01-Mar-90	120000
15	11	Meera	Lalwani	Finance	north	40	11-Dec-07	110000
16	12	Sheetal	Desai	Director	east	80	12-Dec-13	150000
17	13	K. Sita	Narayanan	Personal	south	60	13-Dec-13	85000
18	14	Priya	Shirodkar	Personal	north	60	14-Dec-12	85000
19	15	Aalok	Trivedi	Admin	north	70	01-Mar-83	90000
20	16	Aakash	Dixit	Admin	east	70	01-Mar-83	90000

FIGURE 3.6 VLOOKUP

	A	B	C	D	E	F	G	H	I	J	K	L	M
1													
2	Empcode	1	2	2	3	4	5	5	6	7	8	9	10
3	First Name	Raja	Kuldeep	Suman	Beena	Seema	Deepak	Julie	Neena	Pankaj	Andre	Sujay	Shilpa
4	Last Name	Raymonde	Sharma	Shinde	Mavadia	Ranganathan	Jain	D'Souza	Mukherjee	Sutradhar	Fernendes	Madhrani	Lele
5	Dept	Sales	Admin	Sales	Mktg	R&D	Personal	R&D	R&D	Sales	Mktg	Finance	Admin
6	Region	north	north	south	east	north	east	west	north	north	north	east	west
7	Deptcode	10	70	10	20	30	60	30	30	10	20	40	70
8	Hiredate	01-Jan-16	01-Mar-17	01-Jan-10	24-Nov-12	04-Sep-13	17-Aug-04	04-Sep-06	04-Sep-08	05-Sep-08	06-Sep-08	07-Sep-08	01-Mar-90
9	Salary	125000	40000	100000	70000	120000	79000	71000	71000	85000	90000	85000	120000

FIGURE 3.7 HLOOKUP

VLOOKUP

If we need to get the value of a column from some other file or sheet based on a common field, you may use VLOOKUP. VLOOKUP is a function that searches for a value (lookup value) in the leftmost column of a given database (table array) and returns a value in the same row from a column you specify.

Syntax:

```
VLOOKUP (lookup_value, table_array, col_index_num, range_lookup)
```

You can write this function by using the built-in-function Arguments dialog-box. Click on the Formulas tab and search in the lookup & reference category for VLOOKUP. You will get a function Arguments dialog box, as shown in *Figure 3.8*:

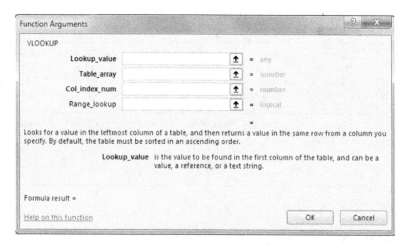

FIGURE 3.8 VLOOKUP Function Argument

The different values to be selected here are as follows:

- *Lookup_value*: The value to be found in the first column of the table. It is the value that you are looking for. Lookup_value can be a value, a reference, or a text string.
- *Table_array*: The table of information in which data is looked up. It is the source database. Use a reference to a range or a range name.
- *Col_index_num*: The column number in table_array from which the matching value must be returned.
- *Range_lookup*: The logical value that specifies whether you want VLOOKUP to find an exact match or an approximate match. If Range Lookup is set as FALSE or 0, VLOOKUP will find an exact match. If the exact match is not found, the error value #N/A is returned. If it is set to TRUE or non-zero, it finds the nearest value that is less than the lookup value.

HLOOKUP

The HLOOKUP function searches for a value in the top row of a table, and then returns a value in the same column from a row you specify.

Syntax:

```
HLOOKUP (lookup_value, table_array, row_index_num,
range_lookup)
```

HLOOKUP works the same way as VLOOKUP. In this case, however, we need to specify the row index number, instead of the column index number.

NOTE *You may also get the function argument box by the following type. Type =VLOOKUP (or =HLOOKUP (as the case may be) and press Ctrl + A.*

Example of VLOOKUP With Range 0 (False):

Suppose you want to add an incentive in the Salary Sheet according to the incentive table, the range of which is A1:B12 in the Incentive worksheet. Follow these steps:

1. Select the cell where you want the result.

2. Click the Insert function. Select the VLOOKUP() function from the Lookup and Reference category.

3. Lookup Value: Select *A2* (The Employee code).

4. Table Array: Select the Incentive Sheet and select the Range from *$A$1:$B$12* (the Employee code and incentive Column).

5. Column Index: Type 2 (Column 2 is the Incentive column in Incentive table).

6. Range Lookup: Type False. (This means we are searching for the exact match from the table for the lookup value).

To remove the #NA (Not Available) error, you can use the function **iferror**. The Syntax of **iferror** is as follows:

```
= iferror (vlookup...., "")
```

Example of VLOOKUP with Range Non-Zero (True)

Suppose you want to add an incentive based on salary slab rates. In this case, instead of using the IF condition, you can use VLOOKUP with a True range. In this scenario, we would create a table, such as *Table 3.2*. In the table array, select this table, and in the field for range lookup, type "True" instead of "False."

TABLE 3.2 Sample Example Table

0	2%
5000	5%
10000	10%
15000	15%

NOTE *The table in this case would be sorted in ascending order of first column.*

Example:

In the Advanced Excel Assignment file titled "emp_inf sheet", we need to retrieve employee information based on employee id. To do this, we may use VLOOKUP, as shown in *Figure 3.9*.

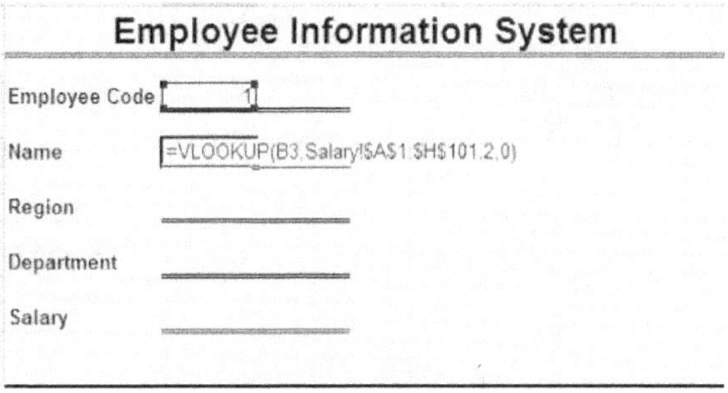

Employee Information System

Employee Code	1
Name	=VLOOKUP(B3,Salary!$A$1:$H$101,2,0)
Region	
Department	
Salary	

FIGURE 3.9 Example of VLOOKUP with Range Non-Zero

To find other details, you may use the same formula and change the column index number accordingly.

MAKING VLOOKUP DYNAMIC

When we have a dynamic database, with new columns frequently being added to the database, the position of the current columns may also change. The column index number of VLOOKUP does not update automatically with the growing database, however. This is why we would need to make VLOOKUP dynamic: in order to pick up the column index number. To do this, we may use one of the following functions to retrieve the column index number dynamically:

- Column
- Match

Using the Column Function in VLOOKUP

To make VLOOKUP dynamic, we can use the column header as an indicator that will dynamically pick up the index number of the particular column in which the required value exists. The syntax for using the column functions in VLOOKUP is:

```
= vlookup (lookup_value, table_array, COLUMN (reference),
Range_lookup)
```

The Reference parameter of the column function will contain the cell reference of the column header from the original database.

Example:

In the preceding example of VLOOKUP, if we need to find the column index number dynamically, we may use the column function, as shown in *Figure 3.10*.

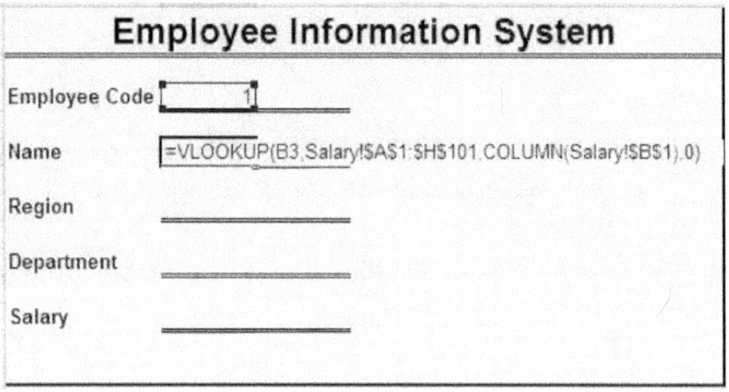

Employee Information System

Employee Code	1
Name	=VLOOKUP(B3,Salary!$A$1:$H$101,COLUMN(Salary!$B$1),0)
Region	
Department	
Salary	

FIGURE 3.10 Using the Column Function in VLOOKUP

B1 is the reference to the column header of the First Name column in the "Salary" worksheet.

Using the Match Function in VLOOKUP

As we saw in the preceding case, we require access to the original database, or at least an idea as to the current position of the column. This information will not always be there for us, however. In that case, we need to use a function that can retrieve the position of the column header by name.

A Match function does the same action. The match function returns the position of a string in a range.

The syntax of the match function is as follows:

```
MATCH (lookup_value, lookup_array, [match_type])
```

The various options to be chosen are:

- *Lookup_Value*: This is the string that we are looking for. It may be a string (for example, "Salary") or a cell reference where the string is stored.
- *Lookup_Array*: This is the range from which we need to know the position of the Lookup_value.

▪ *Match_Type*: This is an optional parameter that is used to specify the type of match we require. We use 0 for Exact match, 1 for Less than, and -1 for Greater Than.

Example:

If we need to find out the position of the string "salary" in the first row of the salary sheet, we would write:

```
=match ("salary", salary! $1:$1, 0)
```

We may use the match function instead of the column index number to get the column index number dynamically.

The syntax of using the match function in VLOOKUP is:

Example:

```
=vlookup (lookup_value, table_array, match (label, firstrow of
source-database, 0), Range_lookup)
```

In the emp_inf example, if we need to make the VLOOKUP more dynamic using the column headers, we may use match with VLOOKUP, as shown in *Figure 3.11*. Here, the match looks for the labels on each field in the header of the salary database and returns the position of the column dynamically.

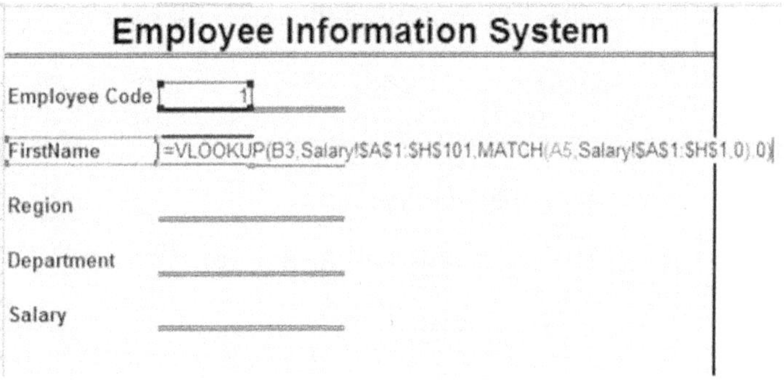

Employee Information System

Employee Code	1
FirstName	=VLOOKUP(B3,Salary!$A$1:$H$101,MATCH(A5,Salary!$A$1:$H$1,0),0)
Region	
Department	
Salary	

FIGURE 3.11 Match Function in Vlookup

INDEX

Sometimes, we need to lookup data based on its row number and column number. The Index function helps us do this.

```
INDEX (array, row_number, [column_number])
```

The syntax of index function is as follows:

As you can see, there are two ways in which you can use the index function. The first syntax is used to look for data in a single database, and the second syntax is used when more than one database is involved.

Example:

Suppose we need to find the data at the intersection of row number 3 and column number 4 of a database. In that case, we may use the following function:

```
=index (database, 3, 4)
```

Index-Match

As we studied before, VLOOKUP looks for data on the basis of values in the first column of the database. If we have a database where our lookup value is in the middle and we need to search towards the left, however, we have to move the column to the left-most corner before we use VLOOKUP. The index function, when used along with match, helps us search for the data even if the lookup value is not present in the left-most column.

```
INDEX (array, [MATCH (lookup_value, lookup_array, [match_
type])],[Match (lookup_value, lookup_array, [match_type])])
```

The syntax for index-match is as follows:

Here, you may use the match function for row number, column number, or both.

Example:

Suppose that from the data given in *Figure 3.12*, we need to find the total sales, given year and quarter. We may then use the function:

```
=INDEX (database, MATCH (qtr 3, column header, 0), MATCH
(year, yearscolumn, 0))
```

| | C11 | | ▼ | fx | =INDEX($A$1:$E$8,MATCH($C$10,$C$1:$C$8,0),MATCH(B11,$A$1:$E$1,0)) | | | | | |

	A	B	C	D	E	F	G	H	I	J	k
1	Qtr 1	Qtr 2	Year	Qtr 3	Qtr 4						
2	179710	256530	2003	238743	298005						
3	200939	248942	2004	208143	254058						
4	215163	196065	2005	225809	161280						
5	178401	296915	2006	172994	282426						
6	248589	150984	2007	146222	273034						
7	162005	105748	2008	230778	224151						
8	291710	213426	2009	244276	141012						
9											
10			2005								
11		Qtr 3	225809								
12		Qtr 4	161280								

FIGURE 3.12 Index-match Function

In *Figure 3.13*, empcode is the third column. If we need to find out the DA or Salary based on the empcode, we normally copy and paste the column towards the left and use VLOOKUP. Instead, we may use index match as given in *Figure 3.13:*

	B10		▼	fx	=INDEX($A$3:$F$7,MATCH($A10,$C$3:$C$7,0),MATCH(B$9,$A$4:$F$4,0))	
	A	B	C	D	E	F	G

	A	B	C	D	E	F	G
1							
2							
3	A	B		C	D	E	
4	Salary	Da	empcode	Hra	Gross	Tax	
5	10	1	2	10	3	4	
6	55	5	3	6	7	8	
7	60	9	4	10	11	12	
8							
9	empcode	DA	Salary	Gross			
10	3	5	55	7			
11	2	1	10	3			
12	4	9	60	11			

FIGURE 3.13 Find the DA or Salary Based on the empcode by Using Index Match

CONCLUSION

In conclusion, the use of formulas and functions in Microsoft Excel is essential for performing calculations, data analysis, and automating tasks. Formulas allow users to combine values, cell references, and operators to perform mathematical calculations, while functions provide predefined formulas for common tasks. By utilizing formulas and functions effectively, users can save time, minimize errors, and perform complex data analysis in Excel. Understanding and mastering these tools is crucial for anyone working with data and spreadsheets in Excel.

EXERCISE

1. Make a copy of the Salary worksheet from the advanced Excel assignment workbook. Calculate the following incentive schemes:

   a. Incentive 1: Everyone working in the Sales department gets 10% of their salary as an incentive; all others get 0%.

   b. Incentive 2: Everyone working in the Sales or Marketing departments gets 5% of their salary as incentive; all others get 2%.

2. Calculate the incentive scheme in Q.1 using VLOOKUP column.

3. Make a column titled "Reporting Manager" after the Salary column and apply the employee code of the managers to the employees, according to their employee numbers as follows, using VLOOKUP.

4

DATA VALIDATION

INTRODUCTION

Sometimes we want to prevent the user from entering a non-text value in a cell. In other words, you can say that you want to restrict the user from entering a certain type of value in the cell. Data Validation does this work for you.

Data Validation is a process which prevents the users from entering invalid data for individual cells or for a cell range. With the help of data validation, you can limit data entry to a specific data type, like integer numbers, fractional (decimal) numbers, or text. You can also set a limit on valid entries.

STRUCTURE

In this chapter, we will go over the following topics:

- Trace Precedents
- Trace Dependents
- Setting Data Validation Rules
- Methods of Data Validation

OBJECTIVES

After studying this chapter, students will be able to describe how to restrict data entry in any cell or in any worksheet, as well as identify various Data Validation techniques.

TRACE PRECEDENTS

Trace Precedents and Trace Dependents are two features in Excel that allow you to visualize and understand the relationships between cells in a spreadsheet. Here is a brief overview of each:

Trace Precedents allow you to see which cells are referenced by a selected cell. This is useful for understanding how data flows through your spreadsheet and identifying any potential errors or issues. To use Trace Precedents, select the cell you want to trace, and then click the Trace Precedents button in the Formula Auditing section of the ribbon. Excel will draw arrows pointing to the cells that are referenced by the selected cell.

For example, imagine you have a spreadsheet that calculates the total revenue for a company based on the number of units sold and the price per unit. The formula for the total revenue is simply the product of the number of units sold and the price per unit. In this example, cell C2 contains the formula for the total revenue, which is "=A2*B2". Cell A2 contains the number of units sold, and cell B2 contains the price per unit.

Refer to *Figure 4.1*:

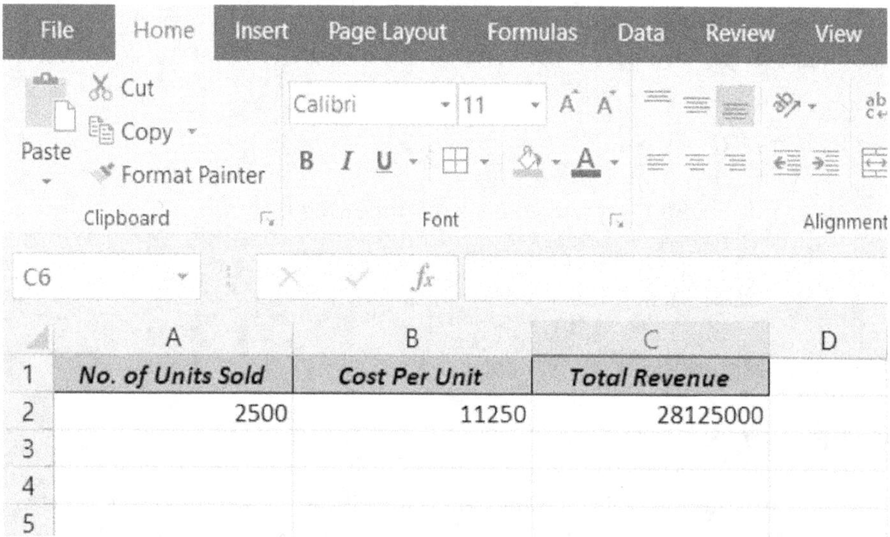

FIGURE 4.1 Example of Trace Precedent

To use Trace Precedents to see which cells are referenced by cell C2, follow these steps:

1. Select cell C2, as shown:

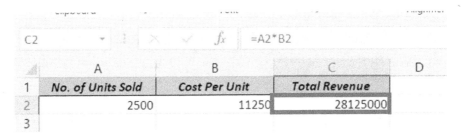

FIGURE 4.2 Apply a Formula for Total Revenue

2. Click on the Trace Precedents button in the Formula Auditing section of the ribbon, as shown:

FIGURE 4.3 Formulas Tab

Excel will draw arrows pointing to cells A2 and B2, indicating that they are the cells referenced by the formula in cell C2, as shown:

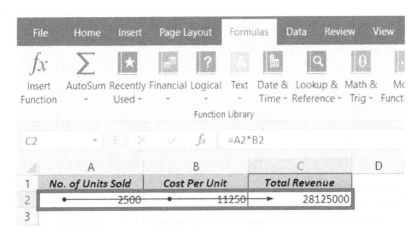

FIGURE 4.4 Trace Precedent

This shows you that the formula in cell C2 is dependent on the values in cells A2 and B2. If you change the values in either of these cells, the value in cell C2 will change accordingly.

Using Trace Precedents helps you understand how data flows through your spreadsheet and is useful for identifying potential errors or issues in your formulas.

TRACE DEPENDENTS

Trace Dependents allows you to see which cells depend on a selected cell. This is useful for understanding the impact that changing a particular cell will have on other parts of your spreadsheet. To use Trace Dependents, select the cell you want to trace, and then click the Trace Dependents button in the Formula Auditing section of the ribbon. Excel will draw arrows pointing to the cells that depend on the selected cell.

Both Trace Precedents and Trace Dependents can help you understand the structure of your spreadsheet and troubleshoot any errors or issues that may arise. By using these features, you can more easily navigate and analyze complex spreadsheets, and make more informed decisions based on your data.

How to Use Trace Dependents

In this example, you have a spreadsheet that calculates the monthly payment on a loan based on the principal, interest rate, and term. The formula for the monthly payment is based on the principle, interest rate, and term, which are stored in cells A1, A2, and A3, respectively. Cell A4 contains the formula for the monthly payment, which is calculated using the PMT function.

To use Trace Dependents to see which cells depend on cell A4:

1. Select cell A4.

2. Click on the Trace Dependents button in the Formula Auditing section of the ribbon.

3. Excel will draw arrows pointing to any cells that depend on cell A4.

4. In this example, cells B4, C4, and D4 depend on cell A4, because they contain the breakdown of the monthly payment, including the portion that goes towards principal, interest, and any additional fees or charges.

Refer to *Figure 4.5*:

FIGURE 4.5 Trace Dependents

By using Trace Dependents, you can see which cells are affected by changing the value in cell A4. If you were to increase the interest rate or change the loan term, for example, you could use Trace Dependents to see how this would affect the monthly payment and its breakdown.

Using Trace Dependents can help you understand the structure of your spreadsheet and make more informed decisions based on your data.

SETTING DATA VALIDATION RULES

Follow the steps below to create a set of rules for data validation:

1. Select the cells for which you want to create a validation rule.

2. On the Data tab, in the Data Tools group, click Data Validation to open the Data Validation dialog box (shown in *Figure 4.1*).

3. Activate the Settings tab.

4. From the Allow list, select a data validation option.

5. From the Data list, select the operator you want.

6. Complete the remaining entries.

7. If required, enter the Input Message in the Input Message tab.

8. If required, enter the error message in the Error Alert tab.

9. Click OK to set the validation rule.

10. Close the dialog box.

Refer to *Figure 4.6*:

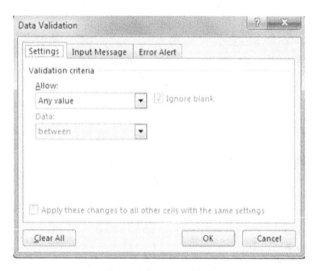

FIGURE 4.6 Data Validation

METHODS OF DATA VALIDATION

Let us now look at a method of data validation: creating a list.

Creating a List

A list is an effective form of data validation where the user is allowed to select an option from a drop-down list which is built into the cell (*Figure 4.7*). The data source may be written manually by the user or selected from the same sheet.

The following are the steps to create a list:

1. Select a blank cell.

2. Select Data tab.

3. Select Data Validation from Data Tool group.

4. Select List.

5. In Source, select the cell with values, or type the data with commas.
   Refer to *Figure 4.7*:

FIGURE 4.7 Creating a List

If the source is from a different sheet, create a named range for all the values and use the name in the Source field for Data Validation.

Allow Numbers Within Limits:

1. In the Allow box, click Whole Number or Decimal.

2. In the Data box, select the type of restriction you want. For example, to set upper and lower limits, select Between.

3. Enter the minimum, maximum, or specific value to allow.

Allow Dates or Times Within a Timeframe:

1. In the Allow box, select Date **or** Time.

2. In the Data box, select the type of restriction you want. For example, to allow dates after a certain day, select Greater Than.

3. Enter the start, end, or specific date or time to allow.

Allow Text of a Specified Length:

1. In the Allow box, click Text Length.

2. In the Data box, click the type of restriction you want. For example, to allow up to a certain number of characters, click less than or equal to.

3. Enter the minimum, maximum, or specific length for the text.

Calculate What is Allowed Based on the Content of Another Cell:

1. In the Allow box, select the type of data you want.

2. In the Data box, select the operator you want.

3. In the box or boxes below the Data box, click the cell that you want to use to specify what is allowed.

For example, to allow entries for an account only if the result will not go over the budget, click Decimal for Allow, select less than or equal to for Data, and in the Maximum box, click the cell that contains the budget amount.

Use a Formula to Calculate What is Allowed:

1. In the Allow box, click Custom.

2. In the Formula box, enter a formula that calculates a logical value (TRUE for valid entries or FALSE for invalid). For example, to give an incentive only if the department is sales and the region is west, you may use the following custom formula: *=and(d2="sales",e2="west")*.

To display an optional input message when the cell is clicked, click the Input Message tab. Ensure the Show Input Message When Cell is Selected checkbox is selected and fill in the title and text for the message.

Specify How You Want Excel to Respond When Invalid Data is Entered:

1. Click the Error Alert tab, and make sure the Show Error Alert After Invalid Data is Entered checkbox is selected.

2. Select one of the following options for the Style box:

   • To display an information message that does not prevent entry of invalid data, select Information.

- To display a warning message that does not prevent entry of invalid data, select Warning.
- To prevent entry of invalid data, select Stop.

3. Fill in the title and text for the message (up to 225 characters).

If you do not enter a title or text, the title defaults to **MS Excel** and the message defaults to "The value you entered is not valid. A user has restricted values that can be entered into this cell."

CONCLUSION

In this chapter, we learned about data validation in Microsoft Excel. Data validation allows us to restrict the type of data that can be entered into cells, ensuring data accuracy and consistency. We explored two methods of data validation: Trace Precedents and Trace Dependents. These features help us understand the relationships between cells and identify potential errors in our formulas.

We also discussed how to set data validation rules using the Data Validation dialog box. This allows us to define specific criteria for the allowed data, such as whole numbers, decimals, dates, times, or text of a specified length. We can even create custom formulas to calculate what data is allowed based on the content of other cells.

Furthermore, we examined the method of creating a list for data validation, which allows users to select an option from a drop-down list. This helps maintain data consistency and simplifies data entry.

EXERCISES

1. Open the Advance Excel Assignment workbook. In the sheet named Validation, do the following data validations.

   a. No duplicates should be allowed in emp_code.

   b. Only text should be allowed in the emp name.

   c. Age should only include numeric data.

   d. Salary should be between 5000 and 50000.

   e. Joining Date should be less than current Date.

2. In the emp_inf sheet create a drop-down list of all the employee codes in cell B3.

5

PROTECTION

INTRODUCTION

In today's digital age, it is paramount to protect sensitive information and ensure data integrity. Microsoft Excel provides a range of features to safeguard your worksheets and workbooks, preventing unauthorized changes and maintaining the confidentiality of your data. In this chapter, we will explore various methods of protection in Excel, allowing you to control access and preserve the integrity of your valuable information.

STRUCTURE

In this chapter, we will go over the following topics:

- Employee information system
- Protecting a worksheet by using passwords
- Protecting a workbook
- Protecting a part of a worksheet
- Protecting a file with a password
- Case study

OBJECTIVES

After studying this chapter, you will understand how to prevent unauthorized changes to your worksheets and how to protect workbooks with passwords.

EMPLOYEE INFORMATION SYSTEM

In the emp_inf example, as shown in *Figure 5.1*, if we wish to use the worksheet as a public template, we will need to prevent unauthorized access to the VLOOKUP formulas. We need to restrict data entry to cell B3. To accomplish these goals, we may use Protection.

Employee Information System	
Employee Code	1 ▾
First Name	Raja Raymondekar
Region	North
Dept	Sales
Salary	15625

FIGURE 5.1 Employee Information System

In Excel, there are three levels of Protection, as shown in *Figure 5.2*.

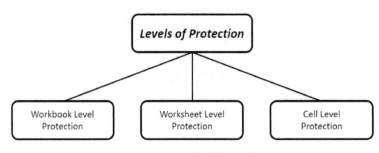

FIGURE 5.2 Levels of Protection

PROTECTING A WORKSHEET BY USING PASSWORDS

Take the following steps to password protect a worksheet:

1. Activate the Review ribbon tab.

2. In the Changes ribbon group, click Protect Sheet to open the Protect Sheet dialog box.

3. Check the options you want.

4. Type a password.

5. Click OK.

6. The Confirm Password dialog box appears.

7. In the Re-enter Password to Proceed box, type the same password to confirm.

8. Click OK to close the password confirmation box and the dialog box.

PROTECTING A WORKBOOK

Workbook level protection can be done in two ways, as shown in *Figure 5.3*.

▪ Protect the workbook structure, preventing changes like worksheets being moved, deleted, inserted, hidden, unhidden, or renamed.
▪ Protect the workbook window and ensure that the window is the same size and position each time it is opened.

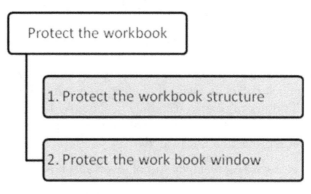

FIGURE 5.3 Protect the Workbook

Perform the following steps to protect a workbook:

1. Activate the Review ribbon tab.

2. In the Changes ribbon group, click Protect Workbook.

3. In the Protect Workbook dialog box which appears, select either or both options (Structure or Windows) as required.

4. To prevent others from removing workbook protection, you can set a password.

5. After specifying options in the Protect Workbook dialog box, click OK. Refer to *Figure 5.4:*

FIGURE 5.4 Protect Structure and Windows

PROTECTING A PART OF A WORKSHEET

When you protect an entire worksheet, all the cells in the worksheet are locked by default. This means that users cannot make changes to any cell in the worksheet. To allow the users to make changes to particular cells, you must unlock the cells manually before protecting the worksheet. This will allow the users to change data only in the unlocked cells. You can hide the formula before protecting the sheet, so that it is not visible to the user after sheet-level protection is activated.

To password protect only part of a worksheet, perform the following steps:

1. Select the range of cells that you want users to be able to modify.

2. Right-click and choose Format Cells to open the Format Cells dialog box.

3. Activate the Protection tab.

4. Clear the Locked check box.

5. Click OK.

Follow steps six to ten if you wish to hide your formulae, or proceed to step eleven directly:

6. Select the range of cells with formulae that you want to hide from users.

7. Right-click and choose Format Cells to open the Format Cells dialog box.

8. Activate the Protection tab.

9. Check the hidden check box along with the locked check box.

10. Click OK.

Continue with step eleven to password protect the worksheet:

11. Activate the Review ribbon tab.

12. In the Changes ribbon group, click Protect Sheet to open the Protect Sheet dialog box.

13. Type a password.

14. Click OK.

15. The Confirm Password dialog box will appear.

16. In the Re-enter password to proceed box, type the same password.

17. Click OK to close both the password confirmation box and the dialog box.

PASSWORD PROTECTING A FILE

You may wish to save your file with a password so that any user will be asked for a password before they can view or modify your file. To do this, follow the steps below:

1. Click on File button.

2. Select Save As.

3. In the Save As dialog box, click on Tools.

4. Then click on General Options, as shown in *Figure 5.5*.

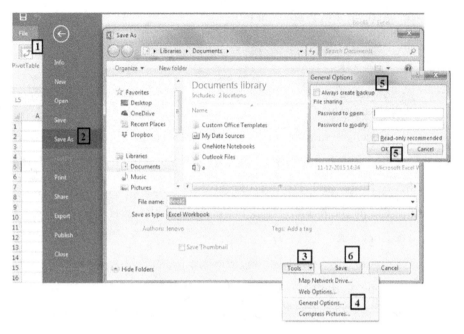

FIGURE 5.5 Protecting a File with a Password

5. Set the password to open or modify, as needed.

6. Save the file.

NOTE   *To use an Excel sheet as a template, save the file with the .xlt extension.*

CONCLUSION

In conclusion, data protection is essential in Microsoft Excel to ensure the security and integrity of your worksheets and workbooks. By utilizing features such as password protection for worksheets, workbooks, and files, you can restrict unauthorized access and prevent unauthorized changes to your data. Additionally, protecting specific parts of a worksheet allows you to control which cells users can modify and will make it easier to maintain data consistency.

EXERCISES

Open the practice folder in the file named *"Practice Assignment Product-Invoice"*. Prepare the invoice template by performing the following steps:

1. In M/s, create a dropdown list of all customer names.

2. The address should be looked up based on the customer name from the "customers" worksheet.

3. The Product column should contain a list of all the products listed in the "product" worksheet.

4. The Rate should be looked up based on the product selected in the adjoining product list.

5. The first "Sr. No" should be entered by the vendor, and the rest should appear only if a product is selected from the product list. See *Figure 5.6*.

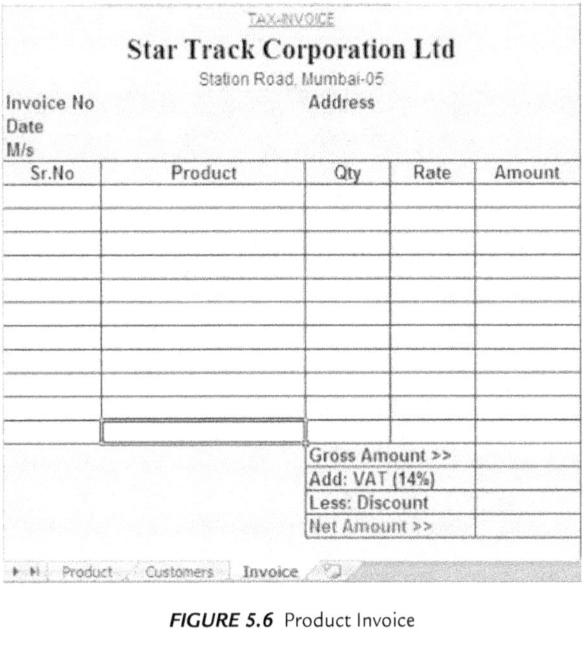

TAX-INVOICE

Star Track Corporation Ltd

Station Road, Mumbai-05

Invoice No				Address	
Date					
M/s					
Sr.No	Product		Qty	Rate	Amount
			Gross Amount >>		
			Add: VAT (14%)		
			Less: Discount		
			Net Amount >>		

▶ ◀ Product Customers Invoice

FIGURE 5.6 Product Invoice

6. The Amount should be calculated as *qty*rate*.

7. The Gross Amount is the sum of all amounts. The Vat is 14% of the gross amount.

8. The Discount should be calculated as 10% of the Gross Amount, if the Gross Amount is greater than 15000.

9. The Net Amount should be calculated as *Gross Amount + Vat-Discount*.

10. Save the file as a template.

NOTE *There should be no visible errors in the template.*

6

Sorting a Database

INTRODUCTION

Sorting data in a database is the process of arranging items in a specific order based on criteria, such as alphabetical or numerical values. It enables easy organization, comparison, and analysis of data, leading to efficient data management and informed decision-making. This chapter explores different sorting techniques, including simple sort, multilevel sort, and customized sort, providing you with the knowledge to effectively arrange and analyze data in your database.

STRUCTURE

In this chapter, we will go over the following topics:

- Definition of sorting
  - Simple sort
  - Multilevel sort
  - Customized sort

OBJECTIVES

After studying this chapter, the readers should be able to define sorting and identify various types of sorting techniques.

DEFINITION OF SORTING

Sorting is any process of arranging items systematically, i.e., arranging items in a sequence ordered by some criterion. For example, sorting data in either increasing or decreasing order.

Simple Sort

To perform a simple sort on a column, follow the following steps:

1. Select any cell in the column which you want to sort.

2. Activate the Data ribbon tab.

3. In the Sort & Filter group, click the Sort Ascending or Sort Descending button. As shown in *Figure 6.1*, this will sort the entire database.

FIGURE 6.1 Simple Sort

Multilevel Sort

Sometimes, you may want to sort your data in multiple columns. For example, you want to sort employee information by region and department. This can be done by multilevel sorting.

To sort a list based on two or more columns:

1. Select any cell in the list.

2. Activate the Data ribbon tab.

3. In the Sort & Filter ribbon group, click Sort to open the Sort dialog box.

4. From the Sort by list, select the column heading of the column by which you want to sort the list, and select a sorting order.

5. All records will be sorted based on the column and the sorting order you selected.

6. From the Then by list, select the next column by which you want to sort.

7. If necessary, add more Then by fields by clicking Add Level.

8. When all Then by fields are complete, click OK, as shown in *Figure 6.2*.

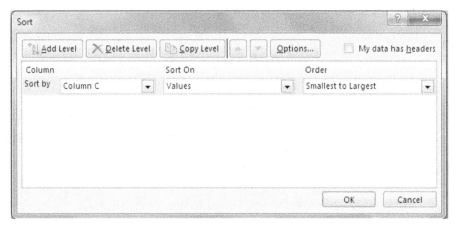

FIGURE 6.2 Multilevel Sort

NOTE *Make sure at least one "Then By" field is selected before clicking on OK button.*

Customized Sort

In custom sorting, the list will sort the data in the sequence specified by you. If we sort the data by region, it sorts either in ascending or descending order, but imagine we want to sort our data in a customized order.

For example, we want to sort North, South, East, and West. To do so, we would need to perform a custom sort, as described in the following steps:

1. Select any cell in the list.

2. Activate the Data tab.

3. In the Sort & Filter group, click Sort to open the Sort dialog box.

4. From the Sort By list, select the column heading of the column by which you want to sort the list.

5. From Sorting Order, select Custom List.

6. It will open the Custom List dialog box.

7. Type the sequence by which you wish to sort.

8. Click the Add button to add the list in custom sort.

9. Click OK.

CONCLUSION

In conclusion, sorting data in a database is essential for organizing information and facilitating efficient analysis. By applying various sorting techniques, such as simple sort, multilevel sort, and customized sort, we can arrange data based on specific criteria and improve the usability and functionality of our database. Sorting enables us to navigate and compare data more effectively, leading to better insights and informed decision-making.

EXERCISES

Refer to *Table 6.1* and answer the questions below.

TABLE 6.1 Database Table

Product	Region	Sales Representative	Sales Revenue	Sales Quantity
Product A	North	John	$10,000	50
Product B	South	Lisa	$8,500	45
Product C	West	Mark	$12,500	65
Product D	East	Sarah	$9,200	48
Product A	West	John	$11,800	60
Product B	North	Lisa	$9,700	52
Product C	East	Mark	$10,300	55
Product D	South	Sarah	$8,900	47
Product A	South	John	$9,500	51
Product B	East	Lisa	$11,200	58
Product C	North	Mark	$10,900	57
Product D	West	Sarah	$12,700	66

1. Sort a sales database in descending order based on sales revenue column.

2. Perform a multilevel sort on a sales database by sorting first by product category in alphabetical order, then by quantity sold in descending order.

3. Customize the sort of a sales database by creating a custom list for product names and sorting based on that list.

4. Sort an inventory database in ascending order based on quantity in stock column.

5. Perform a multilevel sort on an inventory database by sorting first by product category in alphabetical order, then by reorder level in ascending order.

FILTERING A DATABASE

INTRODUCTION

In this chapter, we will explore the topic of filtering a database in Excel. Filtering allows us to display only the rows of information that meet specific criteria, making it easier to analyze and work with large datasets. We will learn about different types of filters, including the AutoFilter feature, number, text, and date filters, as well as the advanced filtering capabilities of Excel. Additionally, we will discover how to filter for unique records in a list. By the end of this chapter, readers will have a clear understanding of how to effectively use filters in Excel to extract and manipulate data based on specific criteria.

STRUCTURE

In this chapter, we will go over the following topics:

- Filters
  - AutoFilter
  - Number, text, or date filters
  - Filtering a list using advanced filter
- Filtering unique records

OBJECTIVES

After studying this chapter, the readers will be able to understand the various types of filters and know how to use them in their worksheet.

FILTERS

At times, you need to display only those rows of information that meet specific criteria. To help you do this, you may use a Filter. Let us discuss more about filters.

AutoFilter

For commonly used criteria, Excel provides the AutoFilter feature. Here is how it works:

1. Select any cell in the list.

2. Activate the Data tab.

3. In the Sort & Filter group, click Filter to display the AutoFilter arrows next to each column heading.

4. From the list, select the column by which you want to filter.

5. Select the criteria.

6. Click OK, as shown in *Figure 7.1*.

FIGURE 7.1 Filter

To clear the filter and show the entire list, click on Filter again. You can filter a list based on more complex criteria by using the Advanced Filtering features. For example, you can display the records of all employees whose salary is between 7000 and 12000.

Excel provides two tools for specifying complex filter criteria:

- Number, text, or date filters
- Advanced filter

Number, Text, or Date Filters

Once you add a filter to data, you also get a Number, Text, or Date Filter option in each field, depending on the type of data in that column. These can be used for field specific filtering like "Begins With" and "Contains" for text fields, "Greater Than,", "Less Than,", and "Between" for number fields, or "Before," and "After" for date fields. Every filter field has a Custom Filter option where you may specify formulas or options other than the ones that are already provided. Refer to *Figure 7.2*.

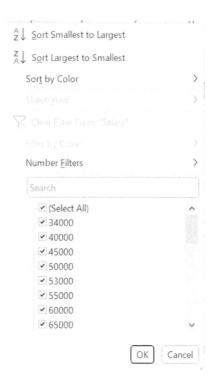

FIGURE 7.2 Number Filter

Refer to *Figure 7.3:*

FIGURE 7.3 Text Filter

Refer to *Figure 7.4:*

FIGURE 7.4 Date Filter

From the dropdown list of the column for which you want to create criteria, choose Text Filters, Date Filters, or Number Filters, then click on Custom to display the Custom AutoFilter dialog box.

1. Enter a comparison criterion below the cell that contains the criteria label. You may use same row for "AND" criteria and different rows for "OR" criteria. For example, the criteria given in *Figure 7.5* can be used to display only records of people in north or south regions.

Criteria Range

	A	B	C	D	E	F	G	H	I
1	Empcode	First Nam	Last Name	Dept	Region	Deptcode	Hiredate	Salary	Salary1
2				Sales	north			>=7000	<=12000
3				Admin	north			>=7000	<=12000
4				Sales	south			>=7000	<=12000
5				Mktg	east			>=7000	<=12000
6				R&D	north			>=7000	<=12000
7				Personal	east			>=7000	<=12000
8				R&D	west			>=7000	<=12000

List Range

	Empcod	First Nan	Last Nan	Dep	Regic	Deptco	Hireda	Salar
2								
3	1	Raja	Raymondeka	Sales	north	10	01-Jan-16	125000
4	2	Kuldeep	Sharma	Admin	north	70	01-Mar-17	40000
5	2	Suman	Shinde	Sales	south	10	01-Jan-10	100000
6	3	Beena	Mavadia	Mktg	east	20	24-Nov-12	70000
7	4	Seema	Ranganathan	R&D	north	30	04-Sep-13	120000
8	5	Deepak	Jain	Personal	east	60	17-Aug-04	79000
9	5	Julie	D'Souza	R&D	west	30	04-Sep-06	71000
10	6	Neena	Mukherjee	R&D	north	30	04-Sep-08	71000
11	7	Pankaj	Sutradhar	Sales	north	10	05-Sep-08	85000
12	8	Andre	Fernendes	Mktg	north	20	06-Sep-08	90000
13	9	Sujay	Madhrani	Finance	east	40	07-Sep-08	85000
14	10	Shilpa	Lele	Admin	west	70	01-Mar-90	120000
15	11	Meera	Lalwani	Finance	north	40	11-Dec-07	110000
16	7	Sheetal	Desai	Director	east	80	12-Dec-13	150000
17	13	K. Sita	Narayanan	Personal	south	60	13-Dec-13	85000
18	14	Priya	Shirodkar	Personal	north	60	14-Dec-12	85000
19	15	Aalok	Trivedi	Admin	north	70	01-Mar-83	90000
20	16	Aakash	Dixit	Admin	east	70	01-Mar-83	90000
21	17	Parvati	Khanna	Mktg	west	20	13-Aug-86	60000
22	18	Farhan	Sadiq	Mktg	north	20	05-Jun-99	34000

FIGURE 7.5 Criteria Range

2. Activate the Data tab.

3. In the Sort & Filter group, click Advanced to open the Advanced Filter dialog box (as shown in *Figure 7.6*).

FIGURE 7.6 Advanced Filter

4. In the List Range box, select the cell range you want to filter. The cell range must include the associated column headings.

Filtering a List Using Advanced Filter

If you wish to filter your data so that it displays only the records of employees of Sales and Admin departments from the north and south regions, who earn between 7000-12000 or 15000-20000, AutoFilter will not serve the purpose. This is because one number filter cannot be applied over another in AutoFilter. The above query requires us to do the same operation on the Salary field. To solve this query, we may have to use Advanced Filter.

While using Advanced Filter, we need to have a criteria range and a list range. The list range is your database.

1. To create a criteria range, we need to make a copy of the column header of the database.

2. In the Criteria Range box, select the cell range that contains your criteria and then click OK.

NOTE *While designing the criteria range, it is better to copy and paste the column header of the entire database as the heading of the criteria range.*

For better visibility, keep the criteria range and list range on different rows. The Advanced Filter command filters your list in place, like AutoFilter, but it does not display drop-down lists for columns. Instead, you have to select the List Range (your data), type criteria in a criteria range on your worksheet, and select the Criteria Range. In the output range, type the cell address where you want to display the output. This is optional.

FILTERING UNIQUE RECORDS

Advanced Filter can also be used to filter out unique values in a list at a separate location. Although the remove duplicates functionality of Excel can help with creating a list of unique values in a list, you would need to copy and paste the unique values if you need them in a different location. To avoid this, use the Advanced Filter option as follows:

1. Select the column or click a cell in the range or list you want to filter.

2. On the Data tab, click Filter.

3. Click Advanced Filter.

4. Do one of the following:

   - To filter the range or list in place, click Filter the list, in-place.
   - To copy the results of the filter to another location, click Copy to another location. Then, in the Copy to box field, enter a cell reference.
   - To select a cell, click Collapse Dialog to temporarily hide the dialog box. Select the cell on the worksheet, then press Expand Dialog.
   - Select the Unique records only check box.

NOTE   *The Advanced filter, copy to option copies to the same worksheet. If you want to copy the filtered data into a different worksheet, select the Advanced Filter command while you are in the worksheet where you want the data to be placed.*

CONCLUSION

Filtering a database in Excel allows us to extract specific information based on criteria we define. In this chapter, we learned about AutoFilter, number, text, and date filters, and advanced filtering. We also explored filtering for unique records. By mastering these techniques, we can efficiently analyze data and make informed decisions. In the next chapter, we will delve into the powerful capabilities of sorting data in Excel.

EXERCISE

1. Open the sheet named Filter. Use AutoFilter to find the records according to following criteria:

    a. People from North or South

    b. People working in Sales or Admin

    c. People working in Sales or Admin, North or South, whose salary is between 7000 and 12000

    d. People working in Sales or Admin, North or South whose salary is between 7000 and 12000 or between 15000 and 20000

SUBTOTALS AND DATA CONSOLIDATION

INTRODUCTION

Sometimes we need to calculate subtotals followed by a grand total at the end of the report. We generally do this by adding a row at the end of each group by using the SUM function. Although this is not an incorrect way to do subtotals, the amount of manual intervention maximizes the possibility of errors.

Excel provides an effective way to do this work with the use of the Subtotal feature. The chapter will wrap up with the consolidation of data.

STRUCTURE

In this chapter, we will go over the following topics:

- Subtotals
- Consolidation of data

OBJECTIVES

After studying this chapter, the reader will be able to define a subtotal, create single and multi-level summaries of data using Subtotal, and identify various types of functions.

SUBTOTALS

The Subtotal functionality of Excel can help us to calculate subtotal and grand total values in a list automatically.

Depending on the type of reporting needed, we have two kinds of work to perform:

- Single Level Subtotal
- Multi-Level Subtotal

Display Subtotal at a Single Level

Before calculating Subtotal on data, we first need sort the list according to the field on which the subtotal needs to be based. Suppose we want to calculate a regional subtotal in the list where we also need to sort data on the basis of the region column. To find the Subtotal, follow the steps below:

1. Click on the Subtotals command from the Data Tab | Outline Group.

2. A Subtotal dialog box will appear, as shown in *Figure 8.1.*

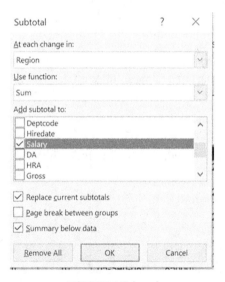

FIGURE 8.1 Subtotal

3. Select the desired column from the At Each Change In list box.

4. Select the function which you want to perform on data from the Use function list box.

5. Select the column on which you want to perform subtotals from the Add Subtotal To: field.

When you click the OK button, Excel inserts a subtotal row for each group of identical items in the selected column. There are a few more options in the Subtotal dialog box, as shown in *Figure 8.1*. These are explained as follows:

- *Choosing a Summary function*: The first time you use the Subtotals command for a list, Excel suggests a summary function based on the type of data in the column you select in the Add Subtotal To box. Choose a different calculation, such as Average, by selecting a different summary function in the Use Function box in the Subtotal dialog box.

- *Choosing the values to summarize*: The first time you use the Subtotals command, the Add Subtotal To box displays the label of the rightmost column. You can leave that label as selected, or you can select the label of any other column in the list. The next time you use the Subtotals command, Excel displays the label of the last column you selected.

- *Displaying subtotal rows above the detailed data*: If you want your subtotal rows to appear above their associated detailed data and the Grand Total row to appear at the top of the list, clear the Summary below the Data check box.

Displaying Nested Subtotal

Sometimes you need to obtain multiple levels of subtotals from data. For example, you may need to group data on Region and then on Dept. In this case, follow the steps below.

1. First, as discussed earlier, you need to sort the data by Region and then by Dept.

2. Click the Subtotals command from the Data Tab | Outline Group.

3. Select the Region column from At Each Change In list box.

4. Select the function which you want to perform on data from the Use function list box.

5. Select the column on which you want to perform subtotals from the Add Subtotal to field.

6. Click the OK button to perform the first level of subtotals.

7. Select the Subtotal command and select the Dept column from At Each Change In list box.

8. Select the function which you want to perform on data from the Use function list box.

9. Select the column on which you want to perform subtotals from the Add Subtotal to field.

10. Clear the Replace the current subtotal check box before you click on the OK button, as shown in *Figure 8.2*.

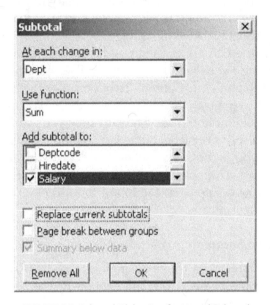

FIGURE 8.2 Subtotal Dialog Box for Nested Subtotal

NOTE   *If you want to copy only the summary details, select the outline where the summary is present. Select the columns required, press Alt (to select only visible cells), then copy and paste it.*

CONSOLIDATE DATA

Consolidating data in Excel allows you to combine data from multiple ranges or worksheets into a single summary report. Below is a step-by-step guide to consolidate data in Excel.

1. Open a new worksheet where you want to consolidate the data, as shown in *Figure 8.3*.

FIGURE 8.3 Open a New Worksheet

2. Select the cell where you want to place the consolidated data, as shown in *Figure 8.4.*

FIGURE 8.4 Select Cell

3. Click on the Data tab in the top menu bar, then click on the Consolidate button in the Data Tools group, as shown in *Figure 8.5.*

FIGURE 8.5 Consolidate Option

4. In the Consolidate dialog box, choose the function you want to use for the consolidation, such as SUM, AVERAGE, COUNT, and so on, as shown in *Figure 8.6*.

FIGURE 8.6 Consolidate Dialog Box

5. Select the range of cells that you want to consolidate by clicking the Collapse Dialog button next to the Reference field, then selecting the cells you want to consolidate. Refer to *Figure 8.7*.

FIGURE 8.7 Selecting the Cells to Consolidate

6. If you want to consolidate data from multiple worksheets, click the Add button in the All References field, and then select the additional worksheet and range of cells you want to consolidate. Refer to *Figure 8.8.*

FIGURE 8.8 Consolidating Data From Multiple Worksheets

7. Repeat the previous step for any additional worksheets you want to include in the consolidation.

8. Make sure that the Top row and Left column checkboxes are unchecked if you do not want to include these items in your consolidation, as shown in *Figure 8.9.*

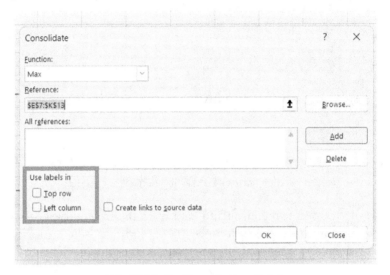

FIGURE 8.9 Checkboxes for Use of Labels

9. Click OK to consolidate the data, as shown in *Figure 8.10.*

FIGURE 8.10 Click OK

After you consolidate the data, the results will be displayed in the cell you selected in the second step. You can also use the Consolidate feature to create pivot tables, which can provide a more detailed summary of your data.

Example of Consolidated Data

Let us say you have three worksheets, each containing sales data for a different region (East, West, and South). Each worksheet has the same format, with columns for Product, Sales Rep, and Sales Amount, as shown in *Figure 8.11*.

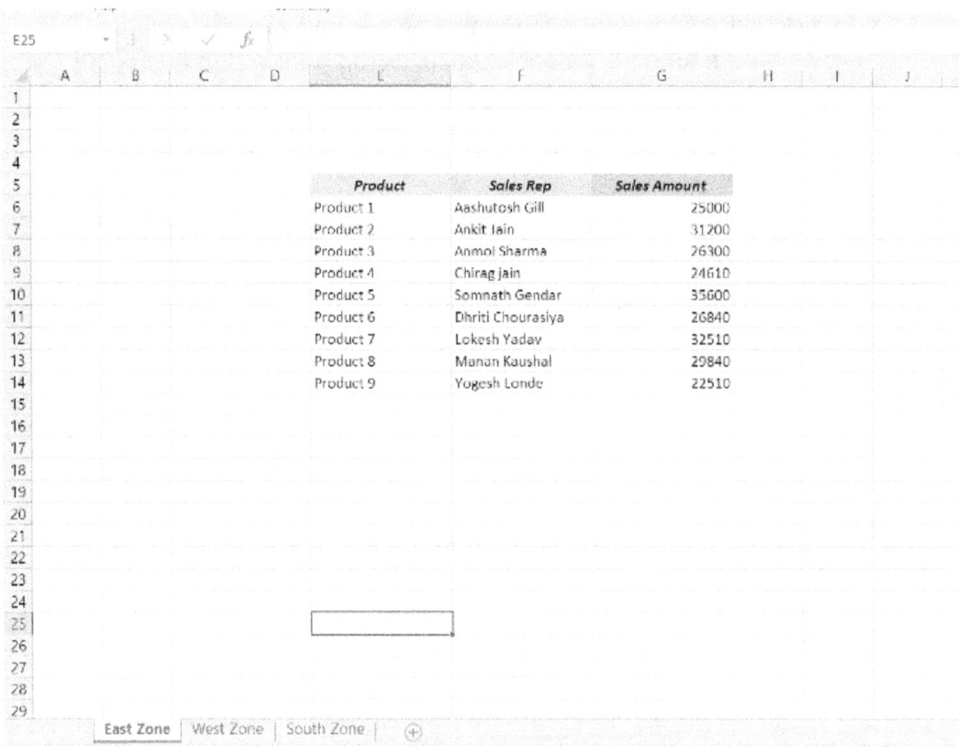

FIGURE 8.11 Sample Worksheets

To consolidate the data from these worksheets into a single summary report, follow the steps below.

1. Open a new worksheet where you want to consolidate the data, as we did in *Figure 8.3*.

2. Select the cell where you want to place the consolidated data, for example, cell A1 as shown in *Figure 8.12*.

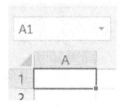

FIGURE 8.12 Select a Cell

3. Click on the Data tab in the top menu bar, and then click on the Consolidate button in the Data Tools group, as was depicted in *Figure 8.5*.

4. In the Consolidate dialog box, choose the function you want to use for the consolidation (e.g., SUM, AVERAGE, COUNT, and so on), as you did in *Figure 8.6*.

5. Select the range of cells that you want to consolidate by clicking the Collapse Dialog button next to the Reference field, and then select the cells you want to consolidate on the East worksheet, for example, A1:C10, as shown in *Figure 8.13*.

FIGURE 8.13 Selecting the Cells to Consolidate

6. If you want to consolidate data from multiple worksheets, click the Add button in the All References field, then select the additional worksheet and range of cells you want to consolidate (for example, select the range on the West worksheet, then select the range on the South worksheet), as shown in *Figure 8.14*.

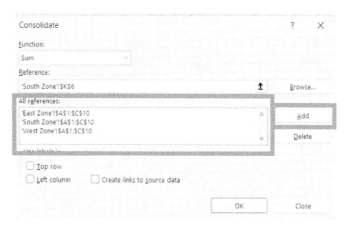

FIGURE 8.14 Consolidating Data From Multiple Worksheets

7. Make sure that the Top row and Left column checkboxes are unchecked if you do not want to include these items in your consolidation, as was shown in *Figure 8.9*.

8. Click OK to consolidate the data, as was shown in *Figure 8.10*.

    The final consolidated data can be seen in *Figure 8.15*.

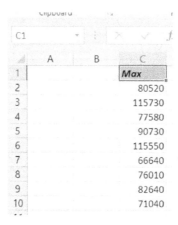

FIGURE 8.15 Final Consolidated Data

CONCLUSION

In conclusion, this chapter introduced the concepts of subtotals and data consolidation in Excel. Subtotals allow for automatic calculation of subtotal and grand total values in a list, making data analysis more efficient. The Subtotal feature can be used to create single-level and multi-level summaries of data based on selected columns and functions.

Data consolidation enables the combination of data from multiple ranges or worksheets into a single summary report. The Consolidate feature provides various consolidation functions and allows for the selection of specific cells or ranges to consolidate. This feature can be especially useful when dealing with data from different sources or worksheets.

By mastering subtotals and data consolidation, users can streamline their data analysis process and generate accurate and comprehensive reports with minimal manual intervention.

EXERCISES

Task 1: Open a new worksheet for consolidation.

Task 2: Calculate subtotals for each region and display them using the Subtotal feature.

Region: East

Product	Sales Rep	Sales Amount
A	John	$500
B	Amy	$700
C	John	$400

TABLE 8.1 Details for East Region

Region: West

Product	Sales Rep	Sales Amount
A	Sarah	$600
B	Sarah	$900
C	Jack	$350

TABLE 8.2 Details for West Region

Region: South

Product	Sales Rep	Sales Amount
A	Emma	$800
B	Emma	$600
C	David	$450

TABLE 8.3 Details for South Region

Task 3: Consolidate the data from all three regions into a single summary report using the Consolidate feature.

Task 4: Answer the following questions:

a. What is the total sales amount for each region?
b. What is the overall sales amount from all three regions?

9

PIVOT TABLES

INTRODUCTION

A pivot table is an interactive, worksheet-based table that quickly summarizes large amounts of data using the format and calculation methods you choose. It is called a pivot table because you can rotate its row and column headings around the core data area to give you different views of the source data. As source data changes, you can update a pivot table. It resides on a worksheet, so you can integrate a pivot table into a larger worksheet model using standard formulas. You can use a pivot table to analyze data in an Excel workbook or from an external database such as MS Access or SQL Server.

STRUCTURE

In this chapter, we will go over the following topics:

- Examining Pivot Tables
- Recommended Pivot Table
- Creating a Pivot Table
- Percent of Grand Total
- Create a Graph Using Pivot Data
- Slicer
- Timeline
- Power View
- Power Pivot
- Benefits of Data Model
- Creating Pivot Tables Using Power Pivot

OBJECTIVES

After studying this chapter, the reader will be able to create pivot tables, make different reports using pivot tables, and use advanced features of pivot tables.

EXAMINING PIVOT TABLES

The data on which a pivot table is based is called the Source Data. Each column represents a field or category of information, which you can assign to different parts of the pivot table to determine how the data is arranged. You can add four types of fields, which are further explained in *Table 9.1.*

TABLE 9.1 Types of Field in Pivot Tables

Field	Description
Report Filter	Filter summarized data in PivotTable. If you select an item in the report filter, the view of PivotTable varies only to display summarized data related to that item. For example, if the area is a report filter, you can display short data for North, West, or all areas.
Row Labels	Row shows items in the field as labels. For example, the row label quarters field contains values, which means that the table shows a line for each quarter.
Column Labels	Column labels are the value of the product field, which means that the table shows a column for each product, in the field that displays the item as a column label.
Σ Values	Summary data are included. These fields usually contain numeric data, such as sales and inventory. The area where the data appears is called the data area.

Refer to *Figure 9.1:*

FIGURE 9.1 Fields of Pivot Tables

Select any cell in a data range that includes a heading for each column in the top row. In the Tables group, click the PivotTable button, or click the PivotTable list and select PivotTable. In the Table/Range box, select the range that contains the data to be used in the pivot table. Select the location for the pivot table. You can place the pivot table in a new or existing worksheet. Click OK to create the pivot table.

You can add fields to a pivot table to specify the data you want to display. The fields of the source data appear in the "PivotTable Field List" task pane. To add fields, drag the relevant field from the top of the PivotTable Field List to one of the four areas at the bottom. You can add more than one field to an area, and you do not need to add all fields to the table.

To display data, use data in Row Labels list and numeric in Values:

1. Activate the Insert tab, to open the Create PivotTable dialog box.

2. Add fields to headings. You need to place at least one field in the S Values area.

After the field is in place, you can filter the information that appears in the table by selecting from the report in the Filter column, the filter rows, or the filter list. For example, you can show all the data values or restrict PivotTable to summarize just a few of them.

RECOMMENDED PIVOT TABLE

Check the recommendations for pivot. To see the recommendations, select the database and click the Insert tab. Click on the recommended pivot table options, as shown in *Figure 9.2.*

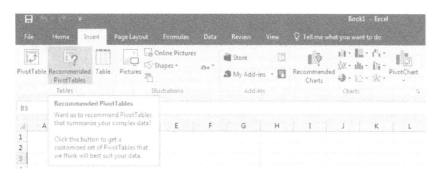

FIGURE 9.2 Recommended Pivot Table

Alternatively, simply select the data to make the pivot table. Click on the button in the lower right corner and select the table option to create the pivot report.

CREATING A PIVOT TABLE

To begin our analysis, we will create a pivot table using the provided sales data. Follow the steps mentioned earlier to set up a pivot table with the necessary fields, including REP, CUSTNAME, PRODUCT, DATE, QTY, CP, S.P., and NET. We will use these fields to analyze the sales data from various perspectives.

Follow the steps below.

1. Select the entire range of data, including headers. You can do this by clicking and dragging your cursor across the data or by using keyboard shortcuts (for example, Ctrl+A). Refer to *Figure 9.3*.

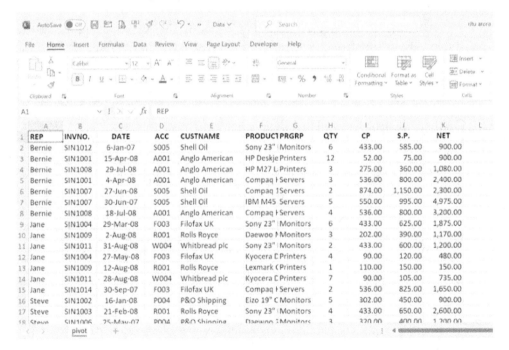

FIGURE 9.3 Sales Data

2. In Excel, go to the **Insert** tab on the ribbon menu, and then click on the PivotTable button, as shown in *Figure 9.4*.

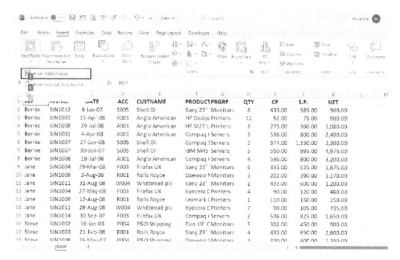

FIGURE 9.4 Insert PivotTable

3. A Create PivotTable dialog box will appear. Ensure that the range of data you selected is correct, then choose where you want to place the pivot table (for example, a new worksheet or an existing worksheet). Refer to *Figure 9.5*.

4. Click OK to create the pivot table.

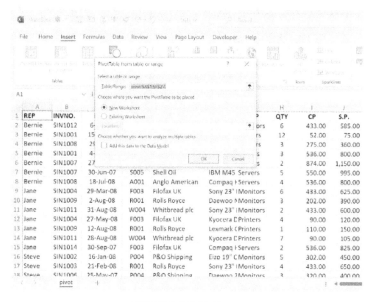

FIGURE 9.5 Table/Range

5. The pivot table field list will appear on the right side of the screen. This list contains the column headers from your sales data. Refer to *Figure 9.6*.

FIGURE 9.6 Customer Quantity

6. Drag and drop the desired fields from the field list into the different areas of the pivot table.

7. Drag the CUSTNAME field to the Rows area to group the data by customer names.

8. Drag the QTY field to the Values area to calculate the total quantity sold. Refer to *Figure 9.7*.

FIGURE 9.7 Value Field Settings

9. You can change the summary function by clicking on the drop-down arrow next to the field name in the "Values" area and selecting a different calculation (for example, average, count). Refer to *Figure 9.8*.

FIGURE 9.8 Sum and Average

PERCENT OF GRAND TOTAL

To find the percent of grand total, follow these steps:

1. Right-click on any value in the Qty column of the pivot table.

2. Select Value Field Settings or Value Settings from the context menu.

3. In the dialog box that appears, choose the option for % of Grand Total or Percentage of the total (exact wording may vary depending on your spreadsheet software).

4. Click OK to apply the calculation.

5. The pivot table will now display the percentage of the grand total for each customer or grouping in the Qty column.

Refer to *Figure 9.9*:

FIGURE 9.9 Percent of Grand Total

Group Items in a Pivot Table

If you want to prepare a report based on the current data for the year or the yearly quarter, then you can use the group option in the pivot table. Follow the steps below.

1. Select any cell in a data range.

2. Activate the Option tab.

3. Click on Group Field.

4. In the By box, click one or more time periods for the groups.

Grouping of Dates

To group dates, follow these steps:

1. Assuming you already have a pivot table created with the Date field in the Rows or Columns area, proceed to the next step.

2. Right-click on any date value in the Date column of the pivot table.

3. In the context menu that appears, select Group or Group Field (the specific wording may vary depending on your spreadsheet software).

4. In the Grouping dialog box, choose the Months option.

5. Click OK to apply the grouping.

6. The pivot table will now display the Date column grouped by month, with each month appearing as a separate item in the pivot table.

   Refer to *Figure 9.10*.

FIGURE 9.10 Grouping of Dates

Monthly Report

The monthly report can be seen in the following *Figure 9.11*.

FIGURE 9.11 Monthly Report

CREATE A GRAPH USING PIVOT DATA

You can use a PivotChart to graphically display data from a PivotTable. A single PivotChart provides different views of the same data. When you create a PivotChart, the row fields of the PivotTable become the categories, and the column fields become the series.

To create a PivotChart, select any cell within a PivotTable, and click Chart in the Tools group on the Options tab. Select Options for the chart as you would for a standard chart, then click OK. You can also create a new PivotChart and PivotTable at the same time by selecting a cell in the source data and selecting PivotChart from the PivotTable list in the Tables group on the Insert tab. Refer to *Figure 9.12*.

FIGURE 9.12 Monthly Chart

To group the Date column in your pivot table by both month and year:

1. Right-click on any date value in the Date column of the pivot table and select Group.

2. In the Grouping dialog box, choose the Months option and the Years option. Finally, click OK to apply the grouping.

Refer to *Figure 9.13*.

FIGURE 9.13 Grouping by Year and Month

To group the Date column in your pivot table by both year and Qtr, follow these steps:

1. Right-click on any date value in the Date column of the pivot table and select Group.

2. In the Grouping dialog box, choose the Qtr option and the Years option. Finally, click OK to apply the grouping. (Qtr1 refers here to January, February, and March.)

Refer to *Figure 9.14*.

FIGURE 9.14 Grouping by Year and Quarter

Weekly Report

If you have grouping on the date field, you can group items by weeks. Click Days in the By box, and make sure that Days is the only time period selected. Then click on seven in the Number of days box.

Refer to *Figure 9.15*.

FIGURE 9.15 Grouping by Day

The pivot table will now display the data grouped by days, allowing you to see the weekly report with data summarized on a daily basis, as shown in *Figure 9.16*.

FIGURE 9.16 Weekly Report

Grouping of Numbers (Creating Slabs)

For grouping of numbers, follow these steps:

1. Right-click on any value in the Net column of the pivot table.

2. From the context menu, select Group or Group Field option. Refer to *Figure 9.17*.

FIGURE 9.17 Grouping by Numbers

3. In the Grouping dialog box, specify the starting value for your grouping slabs. For example, if you want to start with 0, enter 0 in the Starting at field.

4. In the By field, enter the slab size you want to use. In this case, enter 1000.

5. Click OK to apply the grouping.

The pivot table will now display the Net column with values grouped into slabs of 1000. This grouping allows you to analyze the Qty values based on the defined slabs.

SLICER

Slicers are easy-to-use filtering components. They contain a set of buttons that enable you to quickly filter the data in a PivotTable report, without the need to open dropdown lists to find the items that you want to filter. When you use a regular PivotTable report filter to filter multiple items, the filter indicates that multiple items are filtered, but you have to open a dropdown list to find the filtering details. A slicer clearly labels the filter that is applied and provides details so that you can easily understand the data that is displayed in the filtered PivotTable report. Refer to *Figure 9.18*.

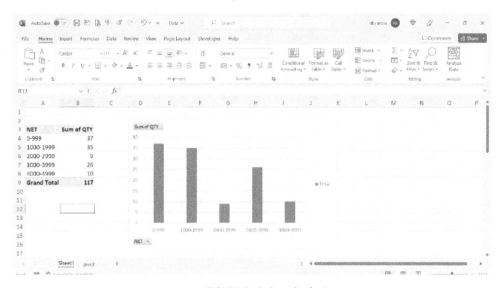

FIGURE 9.18 Grouping by Day

Follow these steps:

1. Select any cell within your pivot table.

2. Go to the PivotTable Analyze or Analyze tab in the Excel ribbon.

3. Locate the Filter group and click on the Insert Slicer button.

4. In the Insert Slicers dialog box, check the box next to Custname to select it. Refer to *Figure 9.19*.

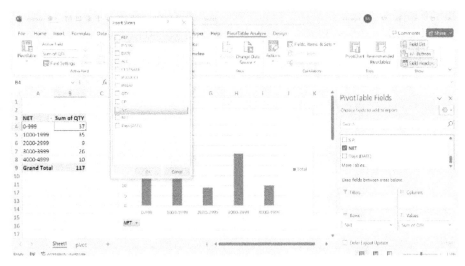

FIGURE 9.19 Slicer

5. Click on the OK button to insert the slicer. Refer to *Figure 9.20*.

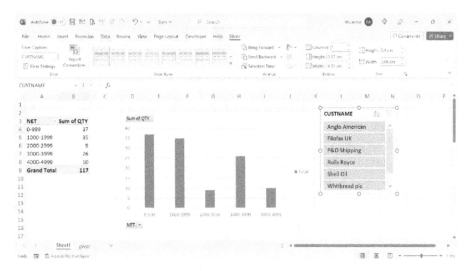

FIGURE 9.20 Customer Slicer

6. A slicer will be added to your worksheet. You can resize and reposition it as needed.

7. Use the slicer to filter the data in your pivot table by selecting the specific Custname values you want to include or exclude.

TIMELINE

Instead of playing around with filters to show dates, you can now use a PivotTable timeline. It is a box you can add to your pivot table that lets you filter by time and zoom in on the period you want. Click Analyze | Insert Timeline to call it up. Refer to *Figure 9.21*.

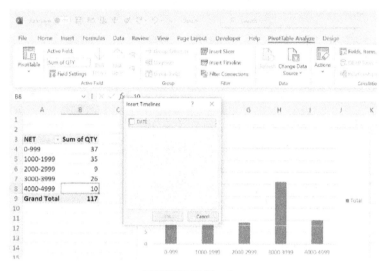

FIGURE 9.21 Timeline

Figure 9.22 shows the date timeline.

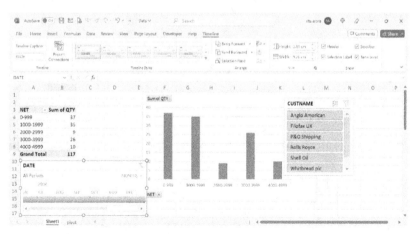

FIGURE 9.22 Date Timeline

POWER VIEW

The Power View add-in allows you to define visually attractive summaries of your worksheet with special emphasis on the variables that you require. With a separate tab, you have the option to view data in the way that best suits you. After defining the relevant power fields, Power View extracts the information from the selected worksheet to give you a complete overview with respect to the viewing filters specified.

Moreover, you can choose a new theme, background, transparency, pictures, and other content with the freedom to insert, modify, arrange, and analyze relationships effectively. Follow the steps below.

1. Select the data.

2. Click on Insert tab.

3. Click on Power View option.

4. You can see the images power view look with Field list with data.

Make use of the filter button, which is on the right side of this data. It will allow you to filter the data as desired with the help of all the column fields.

You can make use of the field list to see various calculations such as sum, min, max, average, and more. Moreover, by using a salary parameter, you can check and see the data according to your selected range. This is the overview of the Power View option.

POWER PIVOT

Power Pivot is an add-in, which we can use to perform powerful data analysis in Excel. The add-in is built into Excel, but it is not enabled. To enable Power Pivot, follow these steps:

1. Go to the File tab.

2. Click on Option | Add-Ins.

3. In the Manage box, click on Com Add-ins.

4. Check the MS Office Power Pivot in COM Add-ins box.

This is a user-friendly way to perform data analysis using familiar Excel features that you already know, such as the Office Fluent user interface, PivotTable and PivotChart views, and slicers. With Power Pivot, we can mash up large volumes of data from various sources, perform information analysis rapidly, and share insights easily.

BENEFITS OF DATA MODEL

In both Excel and PowerPoint, you can create a data model, which is a collection of tables with relationships. The data model, which is seen in a workbook in Excel, is a similar data model that you see in the power pivot window. Any data you import into Excel is available in PowerPoint, and vice versa.

Data Model is a collection of tables and their relationships that reflect real-world relations between business operations and processes; for example, how the product relates to inventory and sales.

Follow the steps below.

1. Convert the data into a table.

2. Import the Excel table into Power Pivot.

   a. The table field list can have more than one table in the pivot table.

   b. We can build the relationships between tables based on one common field so that you do not have to use lookup.

   c. Power view is enabled by Data Model.

CREATING A PIVOT TABLE USING POWER PIVOT

We have four data sets in four different sheets: city, customer, order, and order details. We need to create a city report regarding the total quantity sold. We need to follow these steps:

1. Select the data

   a. Go to the Home tab.

   b. Select the Styles group.

   c. Format as table.

   d. Click on the Design tab.

   e. In the Properties group, give a name to the table.

2. Select the Power Pivot tab.

   a. Go to the Tables group.
   b. Add to Data Model. The table will be added to the data model.

3. Define the relationship

   a. Go to the Home tab in Power Pivot view.
   b. Select the Diagram view from the View tab.
   c. Drag and drop common fields to create the link between two tables.

4. Select Data view in the View tab.

5. Click on Pivot table on the Home tab.

6. Create the pivot table.

7. Choose the field from the table (Active and all). A black border around the table means it is linked with some other table.

8. Select city name from city detail, and quantity from order details.

CONCLUSION

In conclusion, the chapter on pivot tables has provided a comprehensive understanding of this powerful tool in Excel, which can be used for data analysis and reporting. Pivot tables allow users to summarize and analyze large amounts of data quickly and efficiently, providing different perspectives and insights into the data.

The chapter covered various topics, including examining pivot tables, recommended pivot table options, formatting pivot table reports, creating graphs using pivot data, utilizing slicers and timelines for filtering data, and exploring advanced features, such as Power View and Power Pivot.

By following the step-by-step instructions and examples provided in the chapter, readers can learn how to create pivot tables, customize them according to their analysis requirements, and utilize advanced features to enhance their data analysis and reporting capabilities.

Overall, pivot tables offer a flexible and dynamic way to explore and present data, enabling users to gain valuable insights and make informed decisions based on the summarized information. By mastering pivot tables, users can efficiently analyze data, uncover trends, and communicate their findings effectively.

EXERCISES

1. Open the provided Excel spreadsheet containing sales data.

2. Create a pivot table to calculate the total sales revenue for each product category.

3. Format the pivot table to make it visually appealing and easy to read.

4. Create a pivot chart to represent the sales revenue by product category.

5. Create another pivot table to determine the region with the highest sales revenue.

6. Create a pivot chart to visualize the sales revenue by region.

7. Create a pivot table to analyze the monthly sales revenue.

8. Use conditional formatting to highlight any significant changes or trends.

9. Create a pivot table to calculate the average sales revenue per product category.

10

CONDITIONAL FORMATTING

INTRODUCTION

Conditional formatting in Excel allows us to apply formatting rules to cells or ranges based on specific conditions. It helps us highlight important information, visualize data trends, and make our worksheets more visually appealing. In this chapter, we will explore the different types of conditional formatting, such as formatting based on cell values or formulas, working with icon sets, and applying conditional formatting to real-world scenarios using a database case study. By the end of this chapter, you will have a solid understanding of how to use conditional formatting effectively to enhance your data analysis in Excel.

STRUCTURE

In this chapter, we will go over the following topics:

- Conditional formatting
  - Conditional formatting using cell values (column-based conditional formatting)
  - Conditional formatting using formulas (record-based conditional formatting)
- Icon Set
- Formulas with multiple conditions

OBJECTIVES

After studying this chapter, the reader will be able to define conditional formatting and identify the ways to apply conditional formatting. They will also learn how to apply formulas with multiple conditions.

CONDITIONAL FORMATTING

When data needs to be formatted based on certain conditions, we may use conditional formatting. It is easy to highlight cells or a range of cells, emphasize unusual values, and visualize data by using data bars, color scales, or icon sets. *Conditional Formatting* changes the appearance of a cell range, based on a condition (or criterion). If the condition is true, the cell range is formatted based on that condition. If the conditional is false, the cell range is not formatted. Refer to *Figure 10.1*.

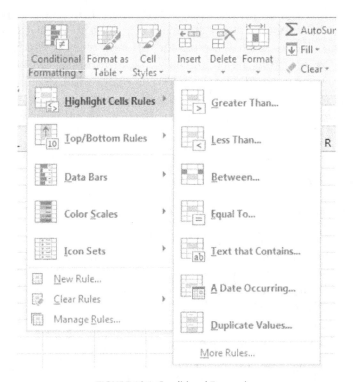

FIGURE 10.1 Conditional Formatting

You can select any of the following types of formatting, as required:

- Format all cells by using a two-color scale.
- Format all cells by using a three-color scale.
- Format all cells by using data bars.
- Format all cells by using an icon set.
- Format only cells that contain text, number, or date or time values.
- Format only top- or bottom-ranked values.
- Format only values that are above or below average.
- Format only unique or duplicate values.
- Compare table columns to determine which cells to format.
- Use a formula to determine which cells to format.
- Clear conditional formats.

For example, you can highlight in green all sales figures that exceed 75,000. Conditional Formatting can be applied based on a cell value or a formula.

NOTE *The area that you select before applying Conditional Formatting determines the area in the worksheet to which the format will be applied.*

Conditional Formatting Using Cell Values (Column-based Conditional Formatting)

To use conditional formatting to apply shading based on cell values, follow the steps below.

1. Select the cells to which you want to apply the Conditional Shading.

2. Activate the Sheet ribbon tab.

3. In the Style group, click Conditional Formatting.

4. From the gallery that appears, select Highlight Cell Rules.

5. From the menu, select a condition for the value in the cell or select More Rules.

6. Specify a condition and cell shading.

7. Click OK to apply the format.

Conditional Formatting Using Formula (Record-based Conditional Formatting)

To apply conditional formatting based on formulas, follow the steps below.

1. Select the cells to which you want to apply the formatting.

2. In the Style ribbon group, click Conditional Formatting.

3. From the menu, select Conditional Formatting Rules Legend to open the Formatting Rules Legend dialog box.

4. Click New Rule to open the Add Formatting Rule dialog box.

5. In the Select a Rule Type box, select Use a formula to determine which cells to format.

6. In the Format Values Where This Formula is True box, enter a formula that evaluates a value to be True or False.

7. Click Format to open the Format Cells dialog box, as shown in *Figure 10.2*.

8. In the Format Cells dialog box, specify the format in which the cells satisfying the condition should appear, and click OK.

9. Click OK to close the Add Formatting Rule dialog box.

10. Click OK to close the Formatting Rules Legend dialog box and apply the format.

NOTE *If the format needs to be applied to the entire database, select the database with or without the header before applying conditional formatting. The formula should be applied to the first row in the selection, however.*

Example:

Figure 10.2 depicts the formula to highlight the records of everyone in the sales department if the selection is made along with the column headers.

If we have selected the database without the header, and want to highlight the records of the person who earns the highest salary, we need to use the following formula:

```
=$h2=max($H$2:$H$101)
```

Refer to *Figure 10.2*.

FIGURE 10.2 New Formatting Rules

ICON SET

In Excel, you have access to more icon sets, including triangles, stars, and boxes. You can also mix and match icons from different sets and more easily hide icons from view. For example, you might choose to show icons only for high profit values and omit them for middle and lower values.

FORMULAS WITH MULTIPLE CONDITIONS

If we want to highlight only the Sales Department from the East region, we can change the formula by following these steps:

1. Select the range without the heading.

2. Click on the Home tab.

3. Select Conditional Formatting.

4. Click on New Rule.

5. Type the formula =AND($D2="Sales",$E2="East")

6. Choose the desired format.

7. Click OK to apply and close.

Apply a Conditional Formula Based on a Different Sheet's Cell Reference

Suppose we want to highlight the records by using the cell reference of another sheet. In that case, follow these steps:

1. Select the entire data without the heading.

2. Click on Home Tab | Conditional Formatting | Manage Rule.

3. Click on New Rule.

4. Select the Rule types as Use a formula to determine which cell to format.

5. In the Edit Rule description, type the formula as: =$D2='cross sheet'!$B$

6. Choose the desired format.

7. Click OK to apply and close the dialog box.

CONCLUSION

In summary, conditional formatting in Excel is a valuable feature that allows us to apply formatting based on specific conditions. It helps us highlight important data, visualize trends, and enhance the presentation of our worksheets. By mastering conditional formatting techniques, we can make our data more visually appealing and gain valuable insights.

EXERCISES

Open the worksheet of Invoice from Excel_Basic from the practice folder and get the result according to the following steps:

1. Get the Type of the customer and Rate using VLOOKUP.

2. Create six copies of the Invoice worksheet and solve the other question.

3. Sort the Record: Retailer or Direct Wholesaler.

4. Filter the Records for June based on sales prices between 3000-5000.

5. Filter the Records for retailer and wholesaler qty between 100-150 and 250-500.

6. Subtotal Records according to Type and customer by Total Qty and Total Amt.

7. Create a summary Report by Month and customer that covers Total Qty/ Total Amt and % of Amt.

8. Highlight the row for Type of customer with the name Direct.

CHAPTER 11

WHAT-IF ANALYSIS

INTRODUCTION

In many situations, you may have to use several different sets of values in one or more formulas in order to explore all the various results. In this case, manual interference may increase, leading to errors. The What-if Analysis tools can come to your rescue in such situations. There are three What-if Analysis tools in Excel, namely:

- Goal Seek
- Data Tables
- Scenario Manager

STRUCTURE

In this chapter, we will go over the following topics:

- Goal Seek
- Projecting figures using a data table
- One-variable data tables
- Two-variable data tables
- What-if Scenarios
- Creating scenarios
- Merging scenarios from another worksheet

OBJECTIVES

After studying this chapter, the reader will be able to understand goal seek, define data tables, and use scenario manager.

GOAL SEEK

Let us assume you have created a formula to calculate PMT. You want to know the number of months you need in order to complete the installment, provided you pay x amount per month. For this kind of reverse analysis, you may use the Goal Seek utility. This type of analysis involves changing the values in a worksheet and observing how these changes affect the results of the formulas. You use Goal Seek to solve problems that have one variable.

The Goal Seek feature in Excel helps us compute a value for the spreadsheet input that makes the value for the given formula match the goal you specify. Goal Seek saves you from performing time-consuming trial-and-error analysis.

USING THE GOAL SEEK COMMAND

To find a specific value that solves a formula, follow the steps below.

1. Select the cell containing the formula.

2. Activate the Data tab.

3. In the Data Tools group, click What-if Analysis and choose Goal Seek to open the Goal Seek dialog box.

4. In the Set cell box, specify the cell that contains the formula you want to solve.

5. In the To Value field, enter the result you want.

6. In the By Changing Cell field, specify the cell that contains the value you want to adjust.

7. Click OK.

For example, a person takes a loan of 100,000 for 36 months, and the EMI [PMT] is 3250. If he pays $5000 per month, in how many months would he complete his payment?

Refer to *Table 11.1*.

TABLE 11.1 Data for Problem

	A	B
1	Loan Amount	100000
2	Rate of Interest	10.50%
3	Payment /month	36
4	PMT [EMI]	($3,250.24)
		PMT(B5/12,B6,B4)

Refer to *Figure 11.1*.

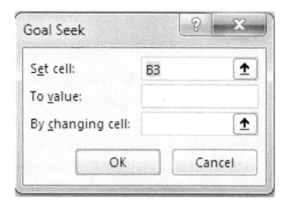

FIGURE 11.1 Goal Seek

PROJECTING FIGURES USING A DATA TABLE

A data table is a range that displays the results when certain values are changed in one or more formulas. The different values you want to enter in a formula are also included in the Data Table. Either a single variable or two variables can be used in the data table.

One-Variable Data Tables

This method is used to observe the effects of changing a single variable in one or more formulas.

Example:

> You can see that when we change the interest rate of monthly payments in the function, PMT (b5/12, 36, 100000) is affected. In this function, A5 is called the input cell, where various input values are substituted from the Data Table. Refer to *Figure 11.2*.

FIGURE 11.2 One-Variable Data Tables Example

> To create a one-variable Data Table, follow these steps:
>
> 1. Enter input values in a row or a column.
>
> 2. If you list the input values in a column, enter the formula in the cell located at the intersection of the row above the first input value and the column to the right of the input values, as shown in *Figure 11.2*. If you list the input values in a row, enter the formula in the cell located at the intersection of the column to the left of the first value and the row, just below the row of input values.
>
> 3. Select the range containing the input values and the formula.
>
> 4. On the Data tab, in the Data Tools group, click What-if Analysis and choose Data Table to open the Table dialog box.
>
> 5. If the input values are in a column, specify the input cell in the Column input cell box. If the input values are in a row, use the Row input cell box.
>
> 6. Click OK.

Two-Variable Data Tables

> You can use a two-variable Data Table to see the effect of changing two variables in one or more formulas, as shown in *Figure 11.3*. For example, you can

see how changing the Loan Amount and the number of payments affects the monthly payment.

To create a two-variable data table, follow the steps below.

1. Enter a formula that contains two input cells.

2. In the same column, below the formula, enter the first list of input values. In the same row, to the right of the formula, enter the second list of input values.

3. Select the range containing both the input values and the formula.

4. In the Data Tools group, click What-if Analysis and choose Data Table to open the Table dialog box.

5. In the Row input cell box, specify the row input cell.

6. In the Column input cell box, specify the column input cell.

7. Click OK.

WHAT-IF SCENARIOS

Scenarios are part of a suite of commands sometimes called What-if Analysis tools. A scenario is a set of values which Excel saves and can substitute automatically in your worksheet. To forecast the outcome of a worksheet model, you can use scenarios. You can create and save different groups of values on a worksheet and switch to any of these new scenarios to view different results. You can define up to 32 changing cells per scenario.

You can use the Scenario Manager for the tasks listed below.

- Create multiple scenarios with multiple sets of changing cells.
- View the results of each scenario on your worksheet.
- Create a summary report of all input values and results.
- Merge scenarios from a group into a single scenario model.
- Protect scenarios from modification and hide scenarios.
- Keep track of modifications with an automatic scenario history.

CREATING SCENARIOS

Let us assume that you have to analyze the net income of a business side-by-side under best, worst, and current circumstances in the following illustration. You may use scenario manager to achieve the required result in a summary format.

You can use the Scenario Manager Dialog box to create scenarios. Follow the steps below.

1. Activate the Data tab.

2. From the What-if Analysis list in the Data Tools group, select Scenario Manager to open the Scenario Manager Dialog box.

3. Click the Add button to open the Add Scenario dialog box.

4. In the Scenario name box, specify the name of the scenario.

5. In the Changing cells box, specify the cells that contain the values you want to change. (for example, select the range of current scenario range).

6. Click OK to open the Scenario Values dialog box.

7. In the Scenario Values dialog box, specify values for the changing cells.

8. Click OK to create the scenario.

If you want to create additional scenarios, click Add again, and then repeat the procedure. When you finish creating scenarios, click OK.

Example:

In the following example, if we need to know the PMT for a range of loan amounts, rates of interest, and number of payments, we may use scenarios, as shown in *Figure 11.3*.

In First Change, the loan amount is 1,50,000, the rate of interest is 10.6%, and the number of terms is 24. In Second Change, the loan amount is 2,00,000, the rate of interest is 11%, and number of payments is 48.

Refer to the following *Figure 11.3*.

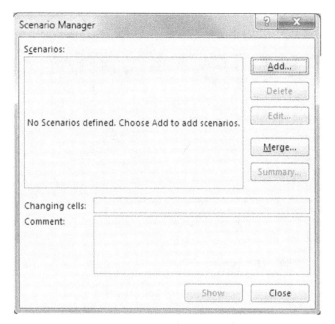

Loan Amount	100000
Rate of Intrest	10.50%
Payment /month	36
PMT [EMI]	($3,250.24)

FIGURE 11.3 Scenario Manager

Create a Scenario Summary Report

To create a scenario summary report, follow these steps:

1. Click on the Summary Scenario Manager dialog box.

2. In the Result cells box, enter the references for the cells that refer to cells whose values are changed by the scenarios (Net Income in the above example). Separate the multiple references with commas, as shown in *Figure 11.4*.

Delete a Scenario

To delete a scenario, follow these steps:

1. Activate the Data tab.

2. From the What-if Analysis list in the Data Tools group, select Scenario Manager to open the Scenario Manager dialog box.

3. Click the name of the scenario you want to delete.

4. Click Delete.

Refer to *Figure 11.4.*

Scenario Summary			
	Current Values:	first change	second change
Changing Cells:			
Loan_Amount	100000	150000	200000
Rate_of_Intrest	10.50%	10.60%	11.00%
Payment_month	36	24	48
Result Cells:			
Loan_Amount	100000	150000	200000
Rate_of_Intrest	10.50%	10.60%	11.00%
Payment_month	36	24	48
PMT_EMI	($3,250.24)	($6,963.35)	($5,169.10)

Notes: Current Values column represents values of changing cells at time Scenario Summary Report was created. Changing cells for each scenario are highlighted in gray.

FIGURE 11.4 Scenario Summary

Display a Scenario

When you display a scenario, you change the values of the cells saved as part of that scenario. Follow the steps below to display a scenario.

1. Activate the Data tab.

2. From the What-if Analysis list in the Data Tools group, select Scenario Manager to open the Scenario Manager dialog box.

3. Click the name of the scenario you want to display.

4. Click Show.

NOTE *Double-clicking the name of the scenario displayed in the Scenarios box is the same as selecting the name and choosing Show values.*

MERGE SCENARIOS FROM ANOTHER WORKSHEET

It is easy to merge scenarios when all What-if models on the worksheets are identical. All changing cells on the source worksheet must refer to the corresponding changing cells on the active worksheet. Excel copies all scenarios on the source sheet to the active worksheet. To merge scenarios from another worksheet, follow these steps:

1. Open all the workbooks that contain the scenarios you want to merge.

2. Switch to the worksheet where you want to merge the scenarios.

3. Activate the Data tab.

4. From the What-if Analysis list in the Data Tools group, select Scenario Manager to open the Scenario Manager dialog box.

5. Click Merge.

6. In the Book box, click a workbook name.

7. In the Sheet box, click the name of a worksheet that contains the scenarios you want to merge.

8. Click OK.

9. Repeat this process if you want to merge scenarios from more worksheets.

Protecting Scenarios

The Add Scenario and Edit Scenario dialog boxes contain two protection options:

- Prevent Changes
- Hide

If you select Prevent Changes and then activate sheet protection, the scenarios you define cannot be edited. This does not prevent you from seeing the values of the changing cells directly on the sheet (unless the cells themselves are locked). Rather, the scenarios themselves are protected from modification when the Prevent Changes checkbox is selected.

In addition, selecting the Hide checkbox removes a scenario name from the list of defined scenarios, preventing its display. Once you select protection options in the Add Scenario or Edit Scenario dialog box, you must activate sheet protection. To do this, use the protection command on the Tools menu, and then choose Protect Sheet.

NOTE   *When sheet protection is activated, you can still add scenarios. You cannot edit or delete them unless the Prevent Changes checkbox is cleared.*

CONCLUSION

In conclusion, the What-if Analysis tools in Excel, including Goal Seek, Data Tables, and Scenario Manager, provide valuable insights and support you in making informed decisions. The tools let you explore different scenarios and analyze the impact of variables on formulas. These tools are essential for financial planning, budgeting, and forecasting, allowing users to save time, reduce errors, and gain valuable insights for better decision-making.

EXERCISES

You work for a financial planning company and are analyzing the impact of different loan options on monthly payments. You have the following information:

Loan Amount: $100,000

Interest Rate: 5.5%

Loan Term: 20 years

Using What-if Analysis, perform the following tasks:

Task 1: Goal Seek

Calculate the monthly payment (EMI) for the given loan amount, interest rate, and loan term.

Use Goal Seek to find the number of months required to pay off the loan if the monthly payment is increased to $800.

Task 2: Data Table

Create a one-variable data table to analyze the impact of changing interest rates (4%, 5%, and 6%) on the monthly payment for the given loan amount and term.

Create a two-variable data table to analyze the impact of changing both the loan amount ($80,000, $100,000, and $120,000) and the loan term (15 years, 20 years, and 25 years) on the monthly payment.

Task 3: Scenario Manager

Create a scenario named "Best Case" with a loan amount of $80,000, an interest rate of 4%, and a loan term of 15 years.

Create a scenario named "Worst Case" with a loan amount of $120,000, an interest rate of 6%, and a loan term of 25 years.

Generate a scenario summary report showing the monthly payment for each scenario.

12

WORKING WITH MULTIPLE WORKSHEETS, WORKBOOKS, AND APPLICATIONS

INTRODUCTION

Working with multiple worksheets, workbooks, and applications is essential for managing and analyzing data effectively. This chapter explores various techniques to establish links between different worksheets, create links between different software, utilize auditing features to trace errors, collaborate in a workgroup, and create hyperlinks for seamless navigation. By mastering these skills, you will be able to enhance your productivity and efficiency in handling complex data scenarios.

STRUCTURE

In this chapter, we will go over the following topics:

- Links between different worksheets
- Creating links between different software
- Auditing features
- Workgroup collaboration
- Creating hyperlinks

OBJECTIVES

After studying this chapter, the reader will be able to identify the various ways to work with multiple worksheets and identify the various ways to work with multiple workbooks and applications.

LINKS BETWEEN DIFFERENT WORKSHEETS

If there is monthly data in different worksheets and we need to have yearly data on a different worksheet, as shown in *Figure 12.1,* we may use intersheet reference.

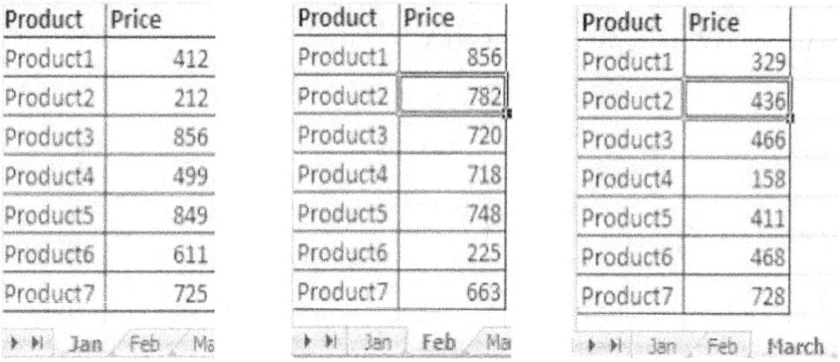

Product	Price
Product1	412
Product2	212
Product3	856
Product4	499
Product5	849
Product6	611
Product7	725

▸ ▶ Jan / Feb / Ma

Product	Price
Product1	856
Product2	782
Product3	720
Product4	718
Product5	748
Product6	225
Product7	663

▸ ▶ Jan / Feb / Ma

Product	Price
Product1	329
Product2	436
Product3	466
Product4	158
Product5	411
Product6	468
Product7	728

▸ ▶ Jan / Feb / March

FIGURE 12.1 Monthly Data

To use a cell reference from a different sheet, you can use the following syntax:

Sheetname!Reference

Figure 12.2 shows an example of finding the sum of cells from a different worksheet:

Product	Price
Product1	=Jan!B2+Feb!B2+March!B2
Product2	1430
Product3	2042
Product4	1375
Product5	2008
Product6	1304
Product7	2116

▸ ▶ Jan / Feb / March / 2011 / ⌐⌐

FIGURE 12.2 Finding the Sum

If the product names are not the same, or are not in the same order, in all the other sheets, this method will not prove useful. In these scenarios, you may use the consolidation feature of Excel, as shown in *Figure 12.3*.

Product	Price
Product1	412
Product2	212
Product5	849
Product6	611
Product7	725

▶ ▸ H Jan / Feb / Ma

Product	Price
Product1	856
Product2	782
Product3	720
Product4	718
Product5	748

▶ ▸ H Jan Feb / Ma

Product	Price
Product1	329
Product2	436
Product3	466
Product4	158
Product5	411
Product6	468
Product7	728

▶ ▸ H Jan / Feb March

FIGURE 12.3 Consolidation Feature

To consolidate data from different worksheets, follow the steps below.

1. Go to the Data Tab.

2. Select Consolidate. The Consolidate dialog box will open, as shown in *Figure 12.4*.

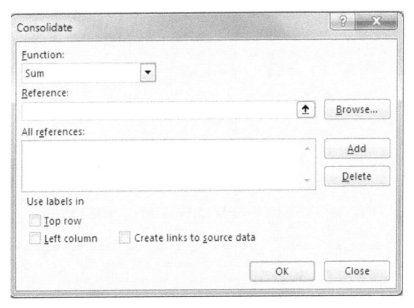

FIGURE 12.4 The Consolidate Dialog Box

3. Select the function you want to apply on the data from the Function drop-down box.

4. Click on Browse and select the first group of data.

5. Click on Add.

6. Repeat the second and third steps for all the data.

7. Click on Top Row and Left Column checkboxes if you want the row and column Title to be picked up.

8. Select Create links to source data, if you wish to have the updated data for every change in the source data.

Refer to *Figure 12.5*.

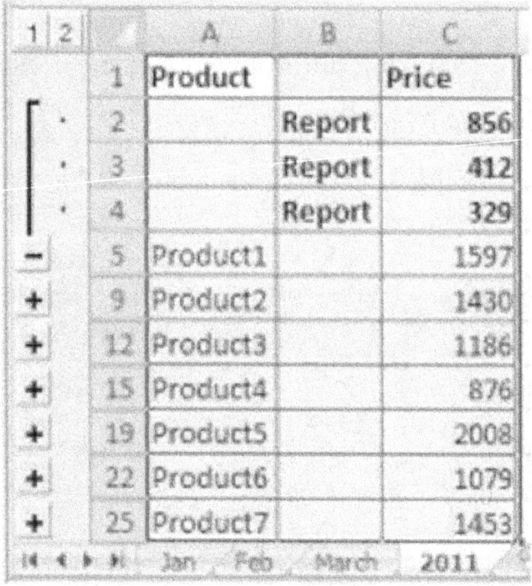

1 2		A	B	C
	1	Product		Price
	2		Report	856
	3		Report	412
	4		Report	329
−	5	Product1		1597
+	9	Product2		1430
+	12	Product3		1186
+	15	Product4		876
+	19	Product5		2008
+	22	Product6		1079
+	25	Product7		1453

Jan Feb March 2011

FIGURE 12.5 Resultant Data

CREATING LINKS BETWEEN DIFFERENT SOFTWARE

Let us assume that we have to copy specific data from an Excel sheet to a Word document. If you do a normal copy and paste, the contents pasted in the Word document are static; they will not be updated even if there is a change of data in the Excel worksheet. Now let us see how to create a link so that the data is updated even in the Word document. Follow these steps:

1. Copy the contents from the Excel worksheet.

2. While pasting in the Word document, click on the Home tab from the clipboard group.

3. Select Edit-Paste special.

4. In the Paste Special dialog box, select the option Paste Link and then select MS Office Word Object Document.

5. Click on OK.

6. Now whenever the data in the Excel worksheet is changed, the change will be automatically reflected in the Word document.

AUDITING FEATURES

You can use the auditing features in Excel to trace errors in a worksheet. You can also trace the relationships between cells and formulas on your worksheets. You might want to identify the cells on which the value of a formula is based. Excel provides the Trace Precedents and Trace Dependents commands to point out such cells.

Dependent and Precedent Cells

A precedent cell provides data to a specific cell. A dependent cell relies on the value of another cell. When you click the Trace Precedents and Trace Dependents buttons in the Formula Auditing ribbon group on the Formulas ribbon tab, Excel draws arrows showing precedent and dependent cells.

WORKGROUP COLLABORATION

Sharing a workbook makes it possible for several members of a workgroup to collaborate on the same set of data. For example, several sales managers could enter their respective regional sales figures in the same workbook, making it unnecessary to collect and consolidate the data manually.

Sharing Workbooks

To share a workbook, follow the steps below.

1. Open the workbook that you want to share.

2. Activate the Review ribbon tab.

3. In the Changes ribbon group, click Share Workbook to open the Share Workbook dialog box.

4. Activate the Editing tab.

5. Check Allow changes by more than one user at the same time, and then click OK.

6. Save the workbook in a location where other users can access it.

You can control how a workbook is shared by using the Advanced tab of the Share Workbook dialog box. For example, under Update changes, you can choose to see other users' changes each time you save the workbook. You can also set the interval at which changes will be shown automatically.

Merging Workbooks

You may need to share a workbook among users who cannot access the same file simultaneously. In such a situation, you can distribute copies of the shared workbook, allow users to make changes to their copies, and then merge those copies into a single workbook. To share a workbook that you intend to merge later, follow these steps:

1. Open the Share Workbook dialog box, activate the Editing tab, and check Allow changes by more than one user at the same time.

2. On the Advanced tab, under Track changes, select Keep change history for. In the box, enter the number of days you want to allow users to make changes in the workbook.

3. Click OK.

4. Make copies of the workbook and distribute one to each user.

After the users have made changes to their copies of the workbook, you can merge the copies into a single workbook, using the following steps:

1. Choose File, Excel Options to open the Excel Options dialog box.

2. Select Customization and add Compare and Merge Workbooks to the Quick Access Toolbar.

3. On the Quick Access Toolbar, choose Compare and Merge Workbooks to open the Select Files to Merge into Current Workbook dialog box.

4. Select the copies of the workbook that contain changes you want to merge.

5. Click OK.

Tracking Changes

You can analyze changes which users have made to a workbook by using the Track Changes feature. This will tell you who made the changes, when they were made, and the original and changed values without having to manually compare the two workbooks. If your workbook is not shared, Excel makes the workbook shared automatically when you turn on the Track Changes feature. To highlight changes, follow these steps:

1. Activate the Review ribbon tab.

2. In the Changes ribbon group, click Track Changes and choose Highlight Changes to open the Highlight Changes dialog box.

3. If the workbook is not shared, check Track changes while editing. If the workbook is shared, this option will be checked by default.

4. Specify how you want the changes to be tracked:

   a. If you want to view changes based on when they were made (for example, after a specific date), check When, then select the necessary setting from the list.

   b. If you want to view the changes made by a specific user, check Who, then select Everyone or Everyone but Me from the list.

   c. If you want to view the changes made to a specific range of cells, check Where, then enter the range.

5. Click OK.

   To review workbook changes and accept or reject them, follow these steps:

1. Open the workbook that contains the tracked changes.

2. Activate the Review ribbon tab.

3. In the Changes ribbon group, click Track Changes and choose Accept or Reject Changes.

4. You will be prompted to save the workbook. Click OK to save the workbook.

5. The Select Changes to Accept or Reject dialog box appears.

6. If you want to view changes based on when they were made, check When and select a time period.

7. Click OK to open the Accept or Reject Changes dialog box.

8. A cell that contains a changed value will be highlighted. This dialog box displays information about each change, including the name of the person who made the change, the date and time it was made, and other changes that will occur if you accept or reject the suggested change. You can scroll down to view the rest of the contents.

9. Click Accept to accept the change or click Reject to restore the original value.

10. The next cell with a changed value will be highlighted.

CREATING HYPERLINKS

To create hyperlinks within the same workbook, follow these steps:

1. To link a particular cell, first name the cell.

2. Select the cell, and click the Formula Tab.

3. Select Define Name.

4. The define name dialogue box will appear.

5. In the Define dialogue box, type a name for the cell and click on Add.

6. Click on Close.

7. Now click on the cell where the hyper link is to be created.

8. Click on Insert Hyperlink or press *Ctrl+K*.

9. The Insert Hyperlink box will appear.

10. Click on the Place in this document option.

11. Click on the Defined name option. The defined names for the workbook will appear.

12. Select the defined name, which we created in the previous step.

13. Click on OK.

14. The link will be created.

Creating Links to a Different File

To create links to a different file, follow these steps:

1. To link a particular cell, first define a name for the cell.

2. Select the cell, then click on the Formula Tab.

3. Select Define Name. The define name dialogue box will appear.

4. In the Define dialogue box, type a name for the cell.

5. Click on Add, then on Close.

6. Now click on the cell where the hyperlink is to be created, and click on Insert Hyperlink or press *Ctrl+K*.

7. The Insert Hyperlink box will appear.

8. Click on Existing file or webpage option.

9. Browse to the folder where you have saved the file you want to link to.

10. Click on the file in the list that appears.

11. The path of the file will appear in the address box under it.

12. Click OK.

You may use this method to link to a webpage, as well. To do this, type the URL of the webpage into the address box. To link to a particular cell in an Excel workbook, do all the steps up to step six in the above process. Add the sheet name and cell reference at the end of the file path in the address box in this format:

File Path#sheetname!Named Range

For example, use c:\test.xlsx#salary!A1 to refer to cell A1 of Salary sheet in the file test.xlsx located in the c drive.

You may also create a new document while creating a hyperlink, or hyperlink to an email address using the options in the hyperlink dialog box.

CONCLUSION

Working with multiple worksheets, workbooks, and applications requires a solid understanding of the available features and techniques. This chapter has provided you with valuable insights into establishing links between worksheets, creating links between different software, utilizing auditing features, collaborating in a workgroup, and creating hyperlinks. By applying these concepts in your day-to- day work, you can streamline your data management processes and improve collaboration with others. With practice, you will become proficient in working with multiple data sources and maximize the potential of your worksheets, workbooks, and applications.

EXERCISES

1. Open an Excel workbook and create three worksheets named "Sales," "Expenses," and "Summary."

2. In the Sales worksheet, enter monthly sales data for different products.

3. In the Expenses worksheet, enter monthly expense data for various categories.

4. Use intersheet referencing to calculate the total sales and total expenses in the Summary worksheet.

5. Consolidate the data from the Sales and Expenses worksheets into a separate worksheet using the consolidation feature.

6. Create a link between an Excel worksheet and a Word document. Copy the consolidated data from the Excel worksheet and paste it into the Word document as a linked object.

7. Use the auditing features offered by Excel to trace precedents and dependents for a specific formula in one of the worksheets.

8. Share the workbook with a colleague and allow simultaneous editing.

9. Merge changes from multiple copies of the workbook back into a single workbook.

10. Track changes made by different users in the workbook and review and accept or reject the changes.

CHAPTER 13

WORKING WITH CHARTS

INTRODUCTION

In this chapter, we will explore the topic of working with charts in Excel. Charts are a powerful tool for visualizing data and presenting it in a meaningful way. By creating charts, you can quickly analyze trends, compare data, and communicate information effectively. This chapter will guide you through the process of creating charts using chart tools, understanding different chart designs, formatting charts, and utilizing recommendations provided by Excel. We will also introduce sparklines, which are compact charts that can be embedded within cells to provide a snapshot of data trends.

STRUCTURE

In this chapter, we will go over the following topics:

- Creating charts using chart tools
- Chart designs
- Formatting charts
- Recommendations
- Sparklines

OBJECTIVES

After studying this chapter, the reader will be able to create a chart using chart tools, identify different types of charts, and format charts.

CREATING CHARTS USING CHART TOOLS

Charts may be used to present data more effectively. For example, it takes time to analyze trends in data, but if it is graphically represented, it will be easier to understand. There are many types of charts, such as column, line, pie, bar, area, and scatter. To create a chart, follow the steps below:

1. Select the data.

2. Go to the Insert tab.

3. From the Charts group, select the chart that you want to create, as shown in *Figure 13.1*.

4. We can select any type of Column chart or click on All Chart Types | Insert Chart. The dialog box will appear.

5. Select the desired chart.

6. Click OK.

7. The chart will be created in the same worksheet. Excel will recommend charts in the dialog box.

   Refer to *Figure 13.1*.

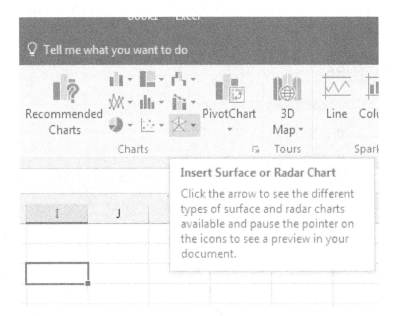

FIGURE 13.1 Charts

CHART DESIGNS

Excel provides different chart designs with every chart type, which we can select from the Design Tab. An example of the Design Gallery can be seen in *Figure 13.2.*

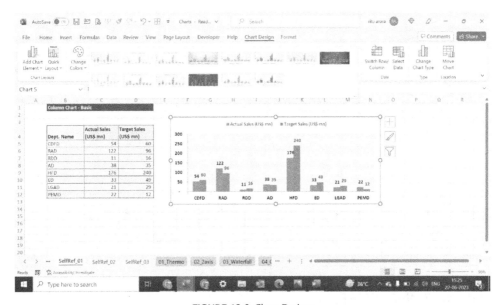

FIGURE 13.2 Chart Designs

Adding Titles and Values in Charts Using Chart Tools

Excel provides some built-in layouts. These can be selected from the Design tab in Chart Tools. The user can also create some custom layouts, and set the Axis Title, Chart Title, Legend, Data Label, and Data Table positions according to their needs.

To do this, follow the steps below.

1. Use the Design Tab. Click on the Add Chart Element option in the Charts Layout Group.

2. Add a Chart Element.

3. Under the Add Chart Element option, there are many options given to the user for formatting the chart, such as adding a secondary axis, adding a name to the axis or to charts, adding a data label, and so on.

Refer to *Figure 13.3*.

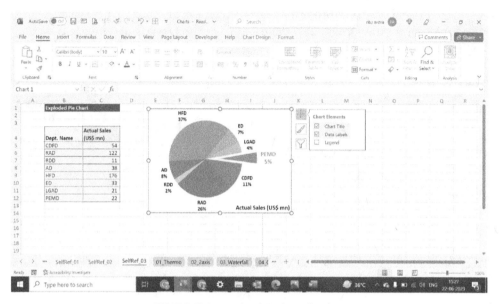

FIGURE 13.3 Associated Options of a Chart

FORMATTING CHARTS

Excel provides a way to change the default color of the various parts of the default design templates.

To do so, use the contextual tab Format under the Chart Tools tab group. It will provide various options to change the outline color, shape alignment, and positioning of the chart.

Charts for Data

According to your needs, you may select different types of charts to represent the data.

Table 13.1 shows various types of data and the charts that can be used to represent them effectively:

TABLE 13.1 Types of Chart

Type of Chart	Data Represented
Column Chart	Represents change in data over a period of time.
Bar Chart	Represents Numerical Comparisons.
Line Chart	Represents evenly spaced values.
Scatter Chart	Displays and compares numeric values, like statistical, scientific, and engineering data.
Pie Chart	Represents associations of different values in a given value.
Doughnut Chart	Represents the relationship of parts to a whole.
Bubble Chart	Represents financial data.
Area Chart	Represents optimum combinations between two sets of data.
Radar Chart	Used when you want to look at several different factors related to one item.

Chart Templates

Sometimes, after creating a chart, we decide to use the same design in the future, as well. This may be difficult to do manually every time. Excel provides a way in which you can save your charts as templates. Perform the following steps to save a chart as a template:

1. After creating the chart, right click on Charts and select the Save as Templates option.

2. The Save as dialog box will appear. Save your chart.

In the future, if you wish to use this template, perform the following steps:

1. Right-click on the newly created chart.

2. A context menu appears. Click on Change Chart Type.

3. In the Insert Chart dialog box, click on Templates. Here, you can see all your saved templates here.

4. Select the required template you want to apply to the current chart.

Chart Filter Option

Another impressive feature is the chart filters option, which lays out all variables (series) and categories for an interactive view when you insert the chart. It can be difficult to filter the chart information. If you want to see only the information you require, make use of the Chart Filter button.

Waterfall Chart

To create a Waterfall Chart in Excel, you can follow these steps:

1. Select the table that includes the category and value data.
2. Go to the Insert tab in the Excel ribbon.
3. In the Charts section, click on the Waterfall chart type.
4. Select the desired Waterfall Chart subtype (for example, "Waterfall" or "Stacked Waterfall").
5. Excel will generate the Waterfall Chart based on the selected data provided in *Figure 13.4*.

Phase	Cost
Material	50,000
Labour	1,00,000
Overhead	2,00,000
Subsidy	(25,000)
Total Cost	3,25,000

FIGURE 13.4 Data Provided for Chart

The Chart can be seen in *Figure 13.5*.

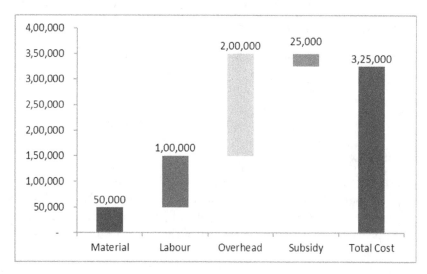

FIGURE 13.5 Waterfall Graph

The resulting Waterfall Chart will display each category as a bar, with positive values represented by bars rising above the starting point and negative values shown as bars going below the starting point. The cumulative total is represented by the length and position of each bar.

RECOMMENDATIONS

The Insert tab is rich with new features, from recommended pivot tables to recommended charts. Excel provides recommendations for achieving the most in the least amount of time. For the best results, use the recommendations offered by Excel.

To use the recommendation, perform the following steps:

1. Select the data to create a chart.

2. Click on the Insert tab.

3. Select Recommended chart options. You will get a view offering various chart types.

4. Select any of the options.

SPARKLINES

Sparklines are tiny charts that fit in a cell. Sparklines helps users to view summary trends alongside data. It takes up a small amount of space. It is especially useful for dashboards or other places where you need to show a snapshot of your business in an easy-to understand visual format without adding much detail. For example, *Figure 13.6* and *Figure 13.7* show how a Sparkline lets you see at a glance how each department performed in May.

	A	B	C	D	E
1	33	32	33	21	
2	16	15	43	36	
3	1	18	58	53	
4	25	50	2	23	
5	45	54	17	9	

FIGURE 13.6 Sparklines Example 1

Refer to *Figure 13.7.*

	A	B	C	D	E
1	33	32	33	21	
2	16	15	43	36	
3	1	18	58	53	
4	25	50	2	23	
5	45	54	17	9	

FIGURE 13.7 Sparklines Example 2

Create a Sparkline

To create Sparklines, follow the steps below.

1. Select an empty cell or a group of empty cells in which you want to insert one or more sparklines.

2. On the Insert tab, in the Sparklines group, click the type of Sparkline that you want to create: Line, Column, or Win/Loss.

3. In the Data box, type the range of the cells that contain the data on which you want to base the earlier scenario.

4. After selecting one or more sparklines, the Sparkline Tools appear and display the Design tab.

5. On the Design tab, you can select one or more of several commands from among the Sparkline, Type, Show/Hide, and Style groups.

6. Use these commands to create a new Sparkline, change its type, format it, show or hide data points on a line Sparkline, or format the vertical axis in a Sparkline group.

Customize Sparklines

After you create sparklines, Excel provides you with options to customize sparklines, such as adjusting the high, low, first, last, or any negative values. You can also change the type of the sparkline into other types, such as Line, Column, or Win/Loss. You can also style from a gallery or set individual formatting options, set options on the vertical axis, and control how empty or zero values are displayed.

Change the Style of Sparklines

Use the Style gallery on the Design tab, which becomes available when you select a cell that contains data. Perform the following steps to change the style of Sparklines:

1. Select a single sparkline or a sparkline group.

2. To apply a predefined style, on the Design tab.

3. In the Style group, click a style, or click the arrow at the lower right corner of the box to see additional styles.

4. Choose a specific formatting for a sparkline.

CONCLUSION

Charts are an essential tool in Excel for presenting data in a visual and easily understandable format. By mastering the techniques discussed in this chapter, you will be able to create, customize, and format charts effectively. Whether you need to analyze trends, compare data, or communicate information to others, charts can greatly enhance the clarity and impact of your data presentations.

EXERCISES

1. Select a set of data from your own spreadsheet or create a sample dataset.

2. Create a column chart using the selected data.

3. Customize the chart by adding titles, legends, and data labels.

4. Apply different chart designs to the created chart and observe the changes.

5. Format the chart by changing colors, outlines, and other formatting options.

6. Save the chart as a template for future use.

7. Use the recommendation feature in Excel to explore different chart options for your dataset.

8. Create a sparkline in a cell to represent a trend within a subset of your data.

9. Customize the sparkline by changing its type, style, and formatting options.

10. Share your chart and sparkline with others to showcase your data analysis and visualization skills.

CREATING AND RECORDING MACROS IN VBA

INTRODUCTION

In this chapter, we will explore the world of VBA macros and their role in automating repetitive tasks in Microsoft Excel. VBA, which stands for Visual Basic for Applications, is a powerful programming language embedded within Excel. Macros, which are sequences of commands, allow us to automate actions and streamline our workflows. Whether you are new to VBA or have some experience, this chapter provides a comprehensive guide to creating and recording macros. You will learn the fundamentals of VBA, the benefits of macros, and how to create macros through writing code or recording actions. Get ready to boost your productivity and efficiency in Excel with the power of VBA macros.

STRUCTURE

In this chapter, we will go over the following topics:

- Introduction to VBA
- Introduction to Macros
- Creating a Macro
- Recording a Macro
- Defining a Macro
- Stop Recording
- Relative Reference Macro
- Running Your Macro
- Running the Macro by Name

OBJECTIVES

This chapter will introduce VBA and macros, explain the process of creating and recording macros, define macros and their properties, demonstrate how to run macros, and provide practical examples for creating macros to automate tasks in Excel.

INTRODUCTION TO VBA

VBA stands for Visual Basic for Applications. It is a programming language that is included with all the Microsoft Office applications, such as Excel, Word, PowerPoint, and so on. It is also the language that Excel macros are written in. VBA is a subset of Microsoft Visual Basic.

Uses of VBA

Some of the uses of VBA are as follows:

- To drive an entire application.
- To combine multiple actions in one action, that is, a macro.
- To write your own functions.

INTRODUCTION TO MACROS

A macro is a series of commands written in logical order, meant to automate any repeated task. It is stored in the Microsoft Visual Basic Module. It can be assigned to the Add-ins tab or to a button on the Quick Access Toolbar.

Below are some examples of how macros are used:

- To automatically add a standard company header to any spreadsheet at the press of a button.
- To format a text file from a general ledger system into a more usable format.
- To print out certain sheets from within a workbook, rather than going through each sheet and printing individually.

CREATING A MACRO

There are two methods used to create macros:

- ▪ *Writing*: Write code for the actions in the sequence using VBA language for the macros.
- ▪ *Recording*: Record your actions in Excel using Macro Recorder. Excel has a Macro Recorder which records the action and writes the code for the macro.

The best approach when it comes to creating a macro is to follow the steps below:

1. Identify the exact problem and the end result that the user wants from the macro.

2. Plan the steps of your macro to obtain the end result successfully.

3. Create your macro either by recording, writing, or combining both.

NOTE   *Record the actions which you have taken in Excel, or write them.*

Adding a Developer Tab on the Ribbon

To add a developer tab on Ribbon, follow these steps:

1. Click on the File Button.

2. Click on the Options… button.

3. On the Customize Ribbon Tab, then select Show Developer Tab in the Ribbon, as shown in *Figure 14.1*.

FIGURE 14.1 Adding Developer Tab on the Ribbon

RECORDING A MACRO

To record a macro, follow these steps:

1. Click on the Developer Tab.

2. In group Code, click on the Record Macro button, as shown in *Figure 14.2*.

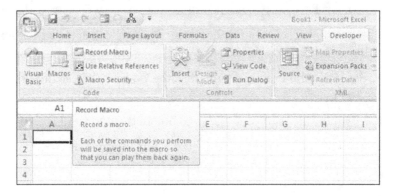

FIGURE 14.2 Recording a Macro

DEFINING A MACRO

To define a macro, follow these steps:

FIGURE 14.3 Defining a Macro

When it comes to assigning names to macros, follow these rules:

- The macro name can consist of letters and numbers.
- It should not start with digits.
- It should not have any special symbol, except underscore (_).
- It can have a maximum of 255 characters.
- Do not use a macro name that is also a cell reference.

Macro Storage

The different macro storage options are as follows:

- *Personal Macro Workbook*: The recording will be performed on the current workbook, and the macro will be stored in a file named Personal.xls. This is a hidden file (located inside the XLSTART folder) which is opened whenever the Excel application is open.
- *This Workbook*: Recording will be performed on the current workbook and the macro will be stored in the current file.
- *New Workbook*: Recording will be performed on the current workbook and the macro will be stored in a new file.

NOTE *Macros can be used if the file in which they are stored is open. If you want a macro to be available whenever you use Excel, select the Personal Macro Workbook option.*

Macro Shortcut

You can use *Ctrl+ Letter* (for lowercase letters) or *Ctrl + Shift+ letter* (for uppercase letters), where *letter* is any letter key on the keyboard. The shortcut key letter you use cannot be a number or a special character, such as @ or #. The shortcut key will override any equivalent default Microsoft Excel shortcut keys while the workbook that contains the macro is open.

Macro Description

The description is used to write details about the macro, such as the purpose of this macro. This helps with post-maintenance.

STOP RECORDING

To stop recording a macro, follow these steps:

1. Perform the actions required to be executed by a macro.

2. Stop recording by either clicking on the Stop Recording button on the Developer tab in the Group Code, or on the status bar at the bottom.

   Refer to *Figure 14.4.*

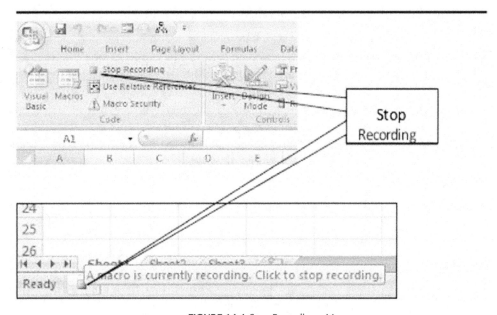

FIGURE 14.4 Stop Recording a Macro

RELATIVE REFERENCE MACRO

If you want the macro to run *relative* to the position of the active cell, record it using relative cell references. On the Developer tab, click on Use Relative Reference so that it is selected. Excel will continue to record macros with relative references until you quit Excel or until you click Use Relative Reference again, so that it is not selected.

Refer to *Figure 14.5.*

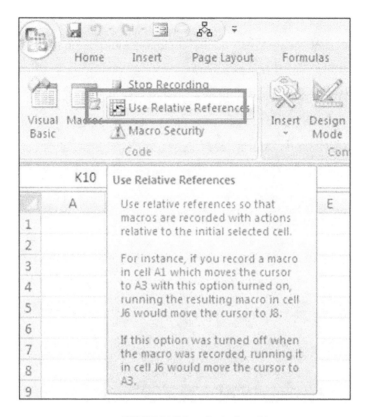

FIGURE 14.5 Stop Recording a Macro

NOTE   *The Use Relative Reference button is a toggle button. Be careful with it, and before you start recording, check whether or not it is selected.*

Scenario 1

Create a macro to automatically add the company's name in a specific format to the first row of any spreadsheet.

For this, refer to Training File1.xls and follow the steps below.

1. Start recording.

2. Add the name "Company_name".

3. Set the shortcut as *Ctrl + Shift + C.*

4. Carry out the following steps:

   a. Select the first cell (since the name should be on the first row).

   b. Type your company's name.

   c. Apply the format: font size 20, bold, blue font, and white background.

   d. Select A1 to H1 cells.

   e. Click on the Merge tool.

5. Stop the recording:

   a. Go to the Tools menu, then click Macro | Stop

Recording. Refer to the following *Figure 14.6*.

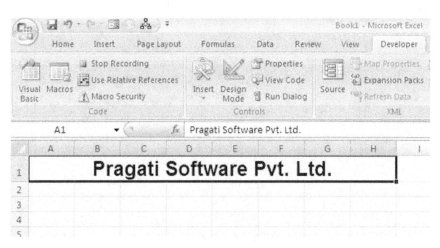

FIGURE 14.6 Scenario 1

RUNNING YOUR MACRO

Macros can be run several ways.

- The shortcut (which you assign while defining the macro)
- The name
- The button on the Quick Access Toolbar
- The button on the worksheet

RUNNING THE MACRO BY NAME

To run your macro by name, follow these steps:

1. Go to the Developer tab.

2. Select Macros (Snapshot 1).

3. Select the macro which you want to run (Snapshot 2).

4. Click on the Run button.

    Refer to *Figure 14.7*.

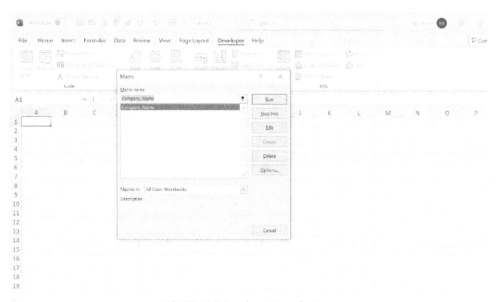

FIGURE 14.7 Running a Macro by Name

Scenario 2

Create a macro to display a product table with the table headers, Product Name, Quantity, Price, Total, and Net. The table must always appear from the second row and first column. Excel should not accept any negative values for price and quantity. This macro will always result from the second row, first column (A1 reference).

Steps to be performed are below. (Refer to Training File1.xls.)

1. Start recording (use name **Product_Table** and shortcut *Ctrl + Shift + P*).

2. Select cell A2 (the table must always appear from the second row and first column).

3. Create a table as per *Figure 14.8*.

4. Write the formula for total and Net Total.

5. Format it.

6. Do validation for quantity and price cells (negative values are restricted).

7. Stop the recording.

Refer to *Figure 14.8*.

Product Name	Quantity	Price	Total
CD			0
Monitor			0
Keyboard			0
Pen Drive			0
Net			0

FIGURE 14.8 Scenario 2

Scenario 3

Create a macro to display the same product table (Scenario 2), but this time it should appear anywhere, wherever the user wants (using relative reference). This macro depends on the user's selection.

The steps to be performed are below:

1. Start recording (use the name Product_Table_Relative and shortcut).

2. Switch on the Relative Reference button on the Stop Recording toolbar.

3. Create a table from the current cell as per *Figure 14.9*.

NOTE *Start typing from wherever you are in the sheet; there is no need to click in the sheet while creating a relative reference macro.*

4. Write the formula for total and Net Total.

5. Format it.

6. Do validation for quantity and price cells (negative values are restricted).

7. Switch off the Relative Reference button.

8. Stop the recording.

   Refer to *Figure 14.9.*

Product Name	Quantity	Price	Total
CD			0
Monitor			0
Keyboard			0
Pen Drive			0
Net			0

FIGURE 14.9 Scenario 3

CONCLUSION

To summarize, this chapter has introduced the fundamentals of VBA macros and their significance in automating tasks in Excel. By creating and recording macros, users can streamline repetitive actions and enhance productivity. Whether through manual coding or the recording feature, macros offer a powerful tool for customizing and optimizing Excel functionality. By leveraging macros, users can save time, reduce errors, and improve efficiency.

EXERCISES

1. Create a macro named "CalculateAverage" that calculates the average of a range of numbers in Excel.

2. Create a macro named "FormatData" that applies specific formatting to a range of cells in Excel.

3. Create a macro named "GenerateReport" that automates the process of generating a report in Excel.

CHAPTER 15

ASSIGNING BUTTONS TO MACROS

INTRODUCTION

In this chapter, we will explore the process of assigning buttons to macros in Excel. By creating buttons on the Quick Access Toolbar and Excel worksheets, we can automate tasks, improve efficiency, and simplify complex operations. Join us as we delve into the world of Excel automation and discover the power of button macro integration.

STRUCTURE

In this chapter, we will go over the following topics:

- Creating buttons on the Quick Access Toolbar
- Modifying menus or buttons
- Creating a button on an Excel worksheet
- Editing the recorded macros

OBJECTIVES

By the end of this chapter, the reader will understand how to create buttons on the Quick Access Toolbar for quick access to macros, and how to modify menus or buttons to customize their appearance and functionality. The reader will also be able to explore the process of creating buttons directly in Excel worksheets for specific tasks, as well as gain proficiency in editing recorded macros to enhance automation and tailor them to specific requirements.

CREATING BUTTONS ON THE QUICK ACCESS TOOLBAR

To create buttons on the Quick Access Toolbar, follow the steps below.

1. Click on the Office button.

2. Click on Excel Options.

3. Go to the Customize Tab.

4. Under the Choose Commands From drop-down box, select Macros.

5. Add your macro to Customize Quick Access Toolbar.

   Refer to *Figure 15.1*.

FIGURE 15.1 Creating Buttons on the Quick Access Toolbar

MODIFYING MENUS OR BUTTONS

Whenever you want to create a new button, edit the existing button, or remove any button from the Quick Access Toolbar, follow the steps below.

1. Click on the Modify… button.

2. Select an icon of your choice.

3. Enter the Display Name.

4. Click OK.

   Refer to *Figure 15.2*.

FIGURE 15.2 Modifying Menus or Buttons

Scenario 4

Create a macro which will extract a region-based sum of the salary (use "Salary worksheet"). On clicking the Subtotal button, a region-based subtotal should be added on a new worksheet, as shown in *Figure 15.3*.

FIGURE 15.3 Scenario 4

For solve this scenario, follow these steps:

1. Start recording (use the name "Subtotal_Macro").

2. Select the Salary sheet (source data).

3. Select cell A1 (the database starts from A1).

4. Perform Sort on Region, as shown in *Figure 15.4*.

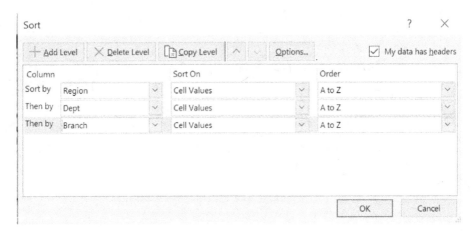

FIGURE 15.4 Scenario 4 Solution

NOTE   *Sorting must be done per the requirement of Subtotal. Incorrect sorting will result in an incorrect subtotal.*

5. Perform Subtotal on Region, as shown in *Figure 15.5*, and follow the steps below.

   a. On Data Tab, go to the Outline Group.

   b. Click on the Subtotal button.

   c. Also select Region in.

   d. Select the Sum function (you can choose any other function per the requirement of your project.)

   e. Select Salary Field.

   f. Click OK.

Refer to *Figure 15.5*.

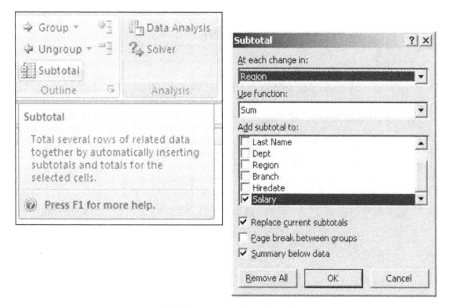

FIGURE 15.5 Scenario 4 Solution

6. Click on Second level of Outline (only the subtotal must be shown).

7. Select the data.

8. Press Alt + ; key combination to select visible cells from the selection.

9. Copy the selection (*Ctrl + C*).

10. Insert the new worksheet (*Shift + F11*).

11. Paste the copied data (*Ctrl + V*).

12. Go to the Salary sheet (source data).

13. Remove Subtotal using the following steps:

    a. Go to Data Tab.

    b. Click Subtotal.

    c. Click on the RemoveAll button.

14. Activate the previous sheet (*Ctrl + PageUp*).

15. Stop recording.

    Refer to *Figure 15.6*.

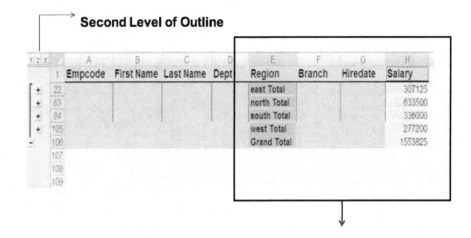

Selection of Visible cells (Alt + ;)

FIGURE 15.6 Scenario 4 Solution

CREATING A BUTTON IN THE EXCEL WORKSHEET

To create a button in the Excel worksheet, follow the steps below.

1. Activate the salary sheet.

2. Go to the Controls Group.

3. Select Button (Form Control), as shown in *Figure 15.7 (b)*.

4. Assign the subtotal_macro, as shown in *Figure 15.7 (c)*.

5. Change the caption (right-click and Edit Text), as shown in *Figure 15.7 (d)*.
   Refer to *Figure 15.7*.

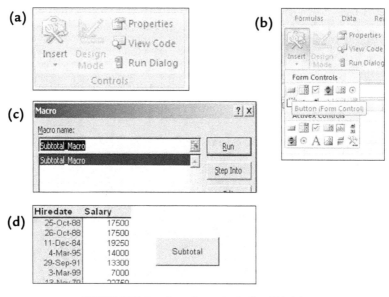

FIGURE 15.7 Creating a Button in the Excel Worksheet

Scenario 5

Create a macro which will extract records from different departments and regions. The user will type the required department and region and click on the filter button, as shown in *Figure 15.8*.

Empcode	First Name	Last Name	Dept	Region	Branch
2	Suman	Shinde	Sales	east	Cuttack
8	Andre	Fernendes	Mktg	east	Darjeeling
11	Meera	Lalwani	Finance	east	Calcutta
15	Aalok	Trivedi	Admin	east	Cuttack
19	Satinder Kaur	Sasan	Mktg	east	Patna
24	Bharat	Shetty	Sales	east	Cuttack
28	Aalam	Qureshi	Personal	east	Patna
39	Kirtikar	Sardesai	Admin	east	Darjeeling
40	Pooja	Gokhale	R&D	east	Calcutta

Dept: Admin   Region: East   Filter

FIGURE 15.8 Scenario 5

NOTE *The above macro will automate the job of Advanced Filter.*

Follow the steps below.

1. Activate the Salary sheet.

2. Create a criteria range for Advanced Filter.

3. Start recording.

4. Use the name "Filter_Macro".

5. Store in this workbook.

6. Click on the heading of the database (cell A5).

7. Do an Advanced Filter.

   a. Click the Data tab.

   b. Click Advanced.

   Refer to *Figure 15.9:*

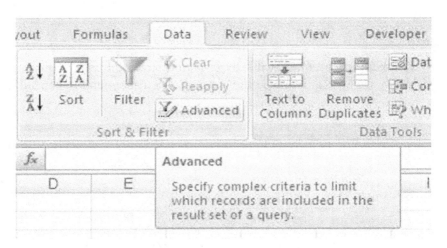

FIGURE 15.9 Scenario 5 Solution

8. Provide List range (database range), as shown in *Figure 15.10*.

9. Provide the Criteria Range.

10. Click OK.

11. Stop Recording.

12. Create a button from Developer Tab | Controls Group.

13. Assign the Filter macro to this button.

Refer to *Figure 15.10*.

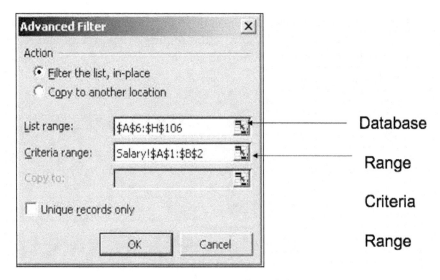

FIGURE 15.10 Scenario 5 Solution

EDITING THE RECORDED MACROS

Sometimes recorded macros may not give you full automation. In these cases, you will have to edit your recorded macros. Alternatively, you might want to add some actions to your recorded macro and then edit your macro.

For example, in Scenario 5, instead of changing criteria in Excel, your macro should ask which region and department to use. The user will type their response, then click OK. The macro will perform the filter.

To edit your recorded macro, follow the steps below.

1. Go to Tools.

2. Click on Macro.

3. Open Visual Basic Editor.

4. Open the code window of your macro.

Scenario 6

Open *Scenario 5* and modify the code to do the following. The user should get an InputBox where they can type the required department and region, then be prompted to click the filter button.

Refer to *Figure 15.11*.

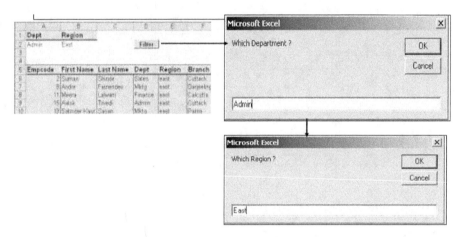

FIGURE 15.11 Scenario 6

To edit your recorded macro, do the following steps:

1. Go to Tools.

2. Select Macro.

3. Select Filter_Macro.

4. Click Edit, as shown in *Figure 15.12*.

5. Open the code window of your macro.

Refer to *Figure 15.12*.

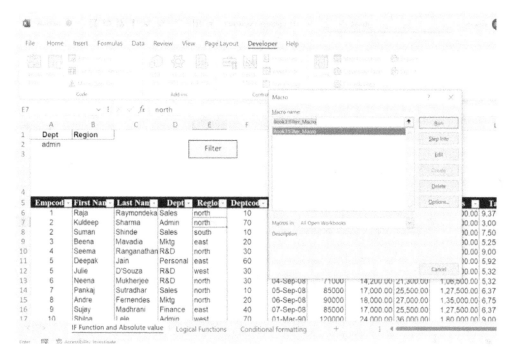

FIGURE 15.12 Scenario 6 Solution

Refer to Training File3.xls.

6. The Macro definition starts with the keyword Sub and ends with the line End Sub.

7. Inputbox is a function used to take input from the end user.

8. Range is a class.

NOTE   *We will discuss writing procedures later in detail.*

Refer to *Figure 15.13*.

Previous code

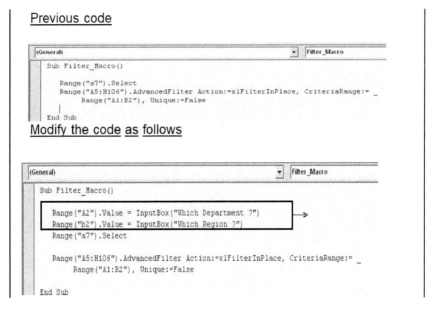

Modify the code as follows

FIGURE 15.13 Scenario 6 Solution

Scenario 7

Create a macro to import data from a txt file (sales.txt) and design a pivot table which shows the sum of sales based on product and month. This macro will automate the import of data from the text file and create a pivot table report (refer to Training File4. xls).

TABLE 15.1 Sample Data

Sum of Sales in Figures		
Product	Month	Total
cd	Jan Feb	100000
	Mar	75000
		12000
cd Total		187000
Monitor Jan Feb		15000
		20000
Monitor Total		35000
Pen Drive	Jan	75000
	Mar	73000
Pen Drive Total		148000
Grand Total		370000

To solve this scenario, follow these steps:

1. Start recording (name the file "import_txt").

2. Click on the Data menu.

3. Select Import External data | Import data.

4. Select sales.txt.

5. Select data type as Delimited, as shown in *Figure 15.14 (1)*.

6. Click Next.

7. Select delimiter (comma), as shown in *Figure 15.14 (2)*.

8. Click Next.

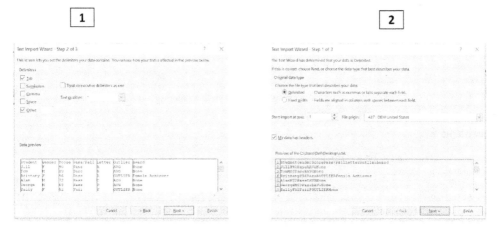

FIGURE 15.14 Scenario 7 Solution

9. Select the type of data, as shown in *Figure 15.15*.

10. Click Finish.

11. Select the existing sheet option, as shown in *Figure 15.15*.

12. Click OK.

13. Create a pivot using imported data and place it in a new worksheet.

14. Stop recording.

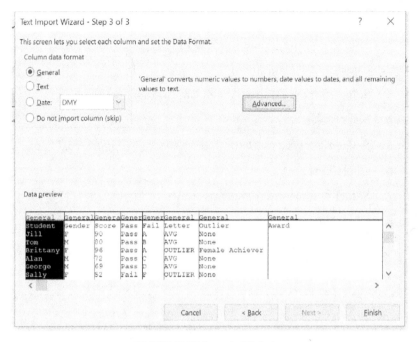

FIGURE 15.15 Scenario 7 Solution

Scenario 8

Refer to Training File4.xls.

Purpose	Original Code	Modified Code
For file selection	ActiveSheet.QueryTables.Ad d(Connection:="TEXT;c:\vb a\sales. txt",Destination:=Ran ge("A1"))	ActiveSheet.QueryTables. Add(Connection:="TEXT;" & Application.GetOpenFilename, Destination:=Range("A1"))
For variable length data	ActiveWorkbook.PivotCache s.Add(SourceType:=xlDatab ase, SourceData:= "Sheet31!R1C1:R7C3"). CreatePivotTable	ActiveWorkbook.PivotCaches.A dd(SourceType:=xlDatabase, SourceData:= Range("a1").CurrentRegion.A ddress).CreatePivotTable

PRACTICE 1

Create a macro (Report_title) which will add a new worksheet with the following details in the existing Workbook cell address cell content.

A2: Your company name A3: Title "Daily report" A4: The date

A6: Sr.No.

B6: Product

C6: Quantity Sold

Follow these steps for the solution:

1. Click on Tools | Macro.

2. Select Record New Macro.

3. Type name of the macro as Report_title.

4. Assign a shortcut key.

5. Select the storage location.

6. Add details in the Description box.

7. Click on OK.

8. Add a blank worksheet (*Shift+F11* or Insert menu | worksheet).

9. Click on A2 and type your company name.

10. Click on A3 and enter "Daily report" for the title.

11. Click on A4 and type "=today()".

12. From A6 to C6, type "Sr. No.", "Product", and "Quantity Sold".

13. Stop recording.

PRACTICE 2

Create a macro to add a signature (your name and designation at the end of the data).

NOTE   *Check that the worksheet is formatted like Practice 1.*

This macro always adds a worksheet before the current worksheet. Modify that macro so that it will add the new worksheet after the current worksheet.

Follow these steps for the solution:

1. Click on Tools | Macro.

2. Select Record New Macro.

3. Enter "summary" as the name of the macro.

4. Assign a shortcut key.

5. Select the location where you want to store the macro.

6. Add details in the Description box.

7. Click on OK.

8. Click on cell A6.

9. Us the *Ctrl + Down Arrow* to reach the end of the data.

10. Click on Relative Reference.

11. Now move three rows down and type your name and designation.

12. Switch off Relative Reference.

13. Stop recording.

14. Modify the statement "Sheets.add" to "sheets.add after:=activesheet".

CONCLUSION

In this chapter, we covered the topic of assigning buttons to macros in Excel. We learned how to create buttons on the Quick Access Toolbar and customize them by modifying menus or buttons. Additionally, we explored the process of creating buttons directly in an Excel worksheet. We also discussed editing recorded macros to enhance their functionality.

EXERCISES

1. Create a macro to extract a region-based sum of salary values and add it to a new worksheet.

2. Create a macro to filter records based on department and region.

3. Import data from a text file and create a pivot table report.

4. Modify the code for file selection and variable length data in existing macros.

5. Practice creating a macro to add a daily report title in a worksheet.

6. Practice creating a macro to add a signature at the end of the data.

CHAPTER 16

FUNCTIONS AND SUBROUTINES IN VBA

INTRODUCTION

The chapter will introduce the concepts of functions and subroutines in Excel VBA programming. It explains the differences between the two and will delve into writing code inside modules using the Visual Basic Editor. The chapter also covers branching techniques to control the flow of code execution within procedures.

STRUCTURE

In this chapter, we will go over the following topics:

- Writing Procedures
- The Visual Basic Editor
- Inserting Modules
- Writing Code Inside a Module
- Sub Procedure
- Function Procedure
- Branching a Procedure

OBJECTIVES

After studying this chapter, the reader will be able to write procedures and understand Visual Basic Editor, which will be used in order to insert modules, write code, and so on. The reader will also learn about sub procedure, function procedure, and branching a procedure.

WRITING PROCEDURES

You can write code for each action that you record. All the procedures are written inside a module.

To write the code, you need to open Visual Basic Editor. The shortcut to open Visual Basic Editor is *Alt + F11*.

A module is a collection of procedures. There are two types of procedures:

- *Sub Procedures:* Sub procedures are used to automate Excel actions. A sub procedure is a unit of code enclosed between the Sub and End Sub block. A sub procedure without any arguments is a macro.
- *Function Procedures:* Functions are used to automate any complex calculations. A Function procedure is enclosed between the Function and End Function block.

The differences between the sub procedures and function procedures are explored in *Table 16.1*.

TABLE 16.1 Differences Between Procedures

Sub Procedure	Function Procedure
It cannot return a value.	It can return a value.
It can perform actions on Excel objects.	It cannot perform actions on Excel objects.

Here are some more points that you can keep in mind:

- Both types of procedure may or may not have arguments.
- A sub procedure with no arguments is a macro.
- All macros are procedures, but not all procedures are macros.

VISUAL BASIC EDITOR

Figure 16.1 shows the Code window in Visual Basic Editor:

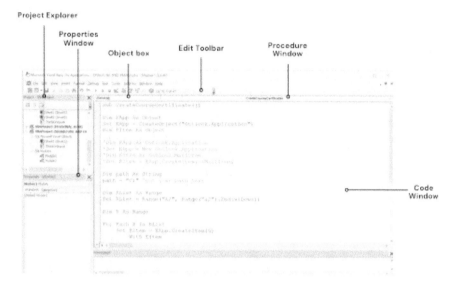

FIGURE 16.1 Code Window in Visual Basic Editor

The different parts in the Code window in Visual Basic Editor are as follows:

- *Project Explorer*: This section displays a hierarchical list of the projects (Excel Workbooks) and all the items contained in and referenced by each project.
- *Properties Window*: This window lists the design-time properties for selected objects and their current settings. You can change these properties at design time. When you select multiple controls, the Properties window contains a list of the properties common to all the selected controls.
- *Code Window*: Use the Code window to write, display, and edit Visual Basic code. You can open as many Code windows as you have modules. You can easily view the code in different forms or modules and copy and paste between them.

Figure 16.2 explores the Project Explorer in more detail.

- *View Code*: Displays the Code window so you can write and edit code associated with the selected item.

- *View Object*: Displays the Object window for the selected item, such as an existing Document or User form.
- *Toggle Folders*: Hides and shows the object folders while still showing the individual items contained within them.
- *List Window*: Lists the loaded projects and the items included in each project.

A Property is a characteristic of any object. The Property Window shown in *Figure 16.2* shows the properties of a selected object.

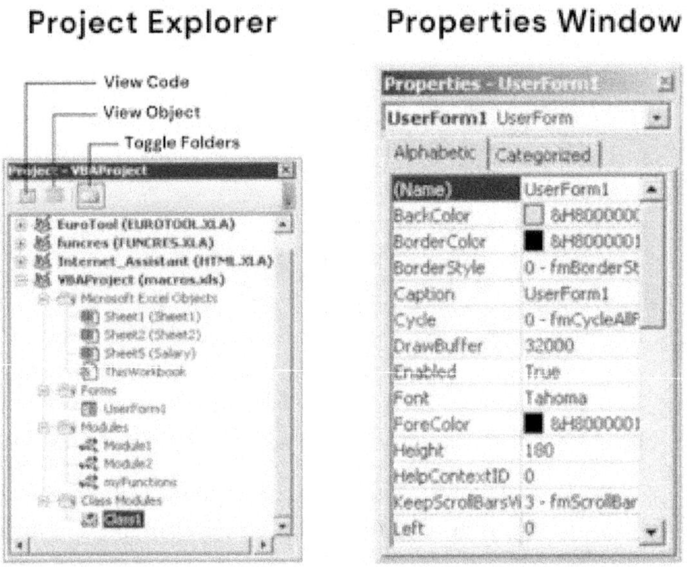

FIGURE 16.2 Project Explorer and the Property Window

Let us now look at the different parts of the Code window (refer to *Figure 16.3*).

- *Object Box*: This view displays a list of objects from current projects.
- *Procedure Window*: This window contains all the procedures of the current module or events of a selected object.
- *Procedure View*: This view displays only one procedure at a time.
- *Full Module View*: This option displays all procedures from the current module.

Refer to *Figure 16.3*.

Code Window

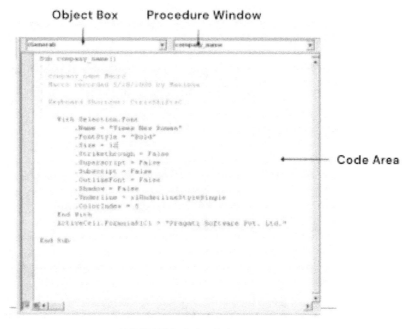

FIGURE 16.3 Code Window

Project Explorer Keyboard Shortcuts

Let us now look at the various keyboard shortcuts:

- ENTER + Æ: Open the selected file from the list, or expand and collapse the list to show its sub-entries.
- SHIFT+ENTERÆ: Open the Code window for the selected file.
- F7 + Æ: Open the Code window for the selected file.
- SHIFT+F10 Æ: View the shortcut menu.
- HOME + Æ: Select the first file in the list.
- END + Æ: Select the last file in the list.
- RIGHT ARROW + Æ: Expands a list, then selects a subentry in the list each time you press it.
- LEFT ARROW + Æ: Selects a subentry in the list, then moves up the list each time you press it until the subentry list collapses into a folder.
- UP ARROW + Æ: Moves up the list one entry at a time.
- DOWN ARROW + Æ: Moves down the list one entry at a time.

INSERTING MODULES

To insert a module, follow the steps below.

1. Select the book in which you want to store your procedures, as shown in *Figure 16.4 (1)*.

2. Select Insert menu, then select Module, as shown in *Figure 16.4 (2)*.

3. Module1 is added. You can change the name through the property window, as shown in *Figure 16.4 (3)*.

   Refer to *Figure 16.4*.

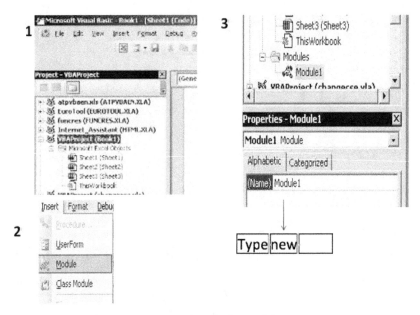

FIGURE 16.4 Inserting Modules

WRITING CODE INSIDE MODULES

To write code inside modules, follow these steps:

1. Double-click the Module inside which you want to write your code for the procedures, as shown in *Figure 16.5 (a)*.

2. Write your code for the procedures, as shown in *Figure 16.5 (b)*. Refer to *Figure 16.5*.

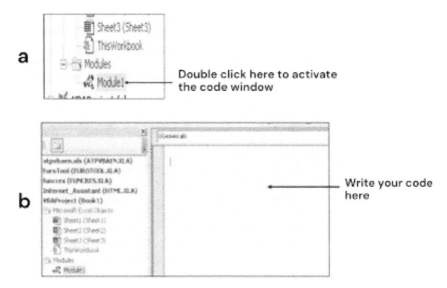

FIGURE 16.5 Writing Code Inside the Module

SUB PROCEDURE

Sub procedure is a series of Visual Basic statements enclosed by the Sub and End Sub statements that perform actions but does not return a value.

A Sub procedure can take arguments, such as constants, variables, or expressions that are passed by a calling procedure.

If a Sub procedure has no arguments, the Sub statement must include an empty set of parentheses.

Macro

The macro is as follows:

```
Sub HelloWorld()
MsgBOx "Hello World"
End Sub
```

Figure 16.6 features a macro.

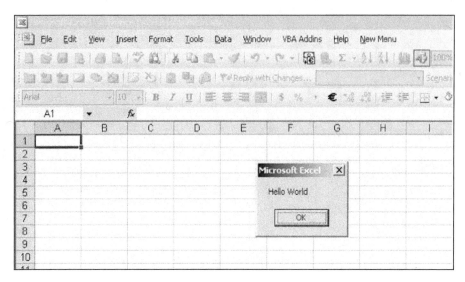

FIGURE 16.6 Macro

FUNCTION PROCEDURE

A Function procedure is a series of Visual Basic statements enclosed by the Function and End Function statements.

A Function procedure is similar to a Sub procedure, but a function can also return a value. A Function procedure can take arguments that are passed to it by a calling procedure.

If a Function procedure has no arguments, its Function statement must include an empty set of parentheses. A function returns a value by assigning a value to its name in one or more statements of the procedure.

For example:

Function Celsius (fDegrees)
```
    Celsius = (fDegrees - 32) * 5 / 9
```
End Function

Refer to *Figure 16.7.*

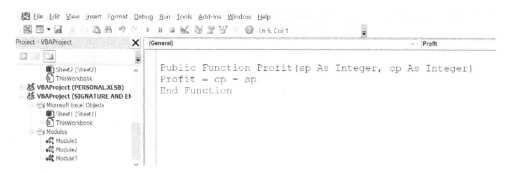

FIGURE 16.7 User-Defined Function

Syntax to Write Functions

Arguments are the inputs you want from the end user to calculate the result.

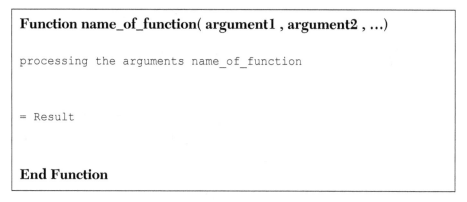

Both procedures may or may not have arguments.

Passing by Value Æ: If you pass an argument by value, the called procedure receives only a copy of the variable passed from the calling procedure. If the called procedure changes the value, the change affects only the copy and not the variable in the calling procedure.

Passing by Reference Æ: If you pass an argument by reference when calling a procedure, the procedure has access to the actual variable in memory. As a result, the variable's value can be changed by the procedure. By default, arguments are by reference.

Scenario 9

Write a function to calculate Profit where profit is the difference of Selling price and Cost price. The Profit function requires two arguments: cost price and selling price.

```
Function Profit(CP, SP)
Profit = SP - CP
End Function
```

Refer to Training File5.xls.

BRANCHING A PROCEDURE

If you want to run a block of code depending on the value of a condition, you can use the following decision structures.

- ¾ If...Then...Endif
- ¾ If...Then...Else...Endif
- ¾ If...Then...Elseif...Then...Else...Endif
- ¾ Select Case ...End Select

Use If...Then...Endif

A single condition that runs a single statement or a block of statements.

Use If...Then...Else...Endif

A single condition that runs two different statements or a block of statements, depending on the result of the condition.

Use If...Then...Elseif...Then...Else...Endif OR Select Case... End

This structure selects more than one condition and runs one of several statement blocks.

Scenario 10

Write a function to check whether a person is eligible to vote or not. To check eligibility, the Vote function requires age as an argument.

Function Vote(Age)
```
If Age >= 18 Then
    Vote = "Eligible"
Else
    Vote = "not eligible"
EndIf
```
End Function

Refer to Training File5.xls.

Scenario 11

Write a function to find the grade of an employee based on basic salary as per the given criteria (Using If Elseif):

Grade Salary

D <8000

C 8000 – 15000

B 15000 – 25000

A >=25000

Function Grade (salary)
```
If salary<8000 Then
    Grade = "D"
ElseIf salary<15000 Then
    Grade = "C"
ElseIf salary<25000 Then
    Grade = "B"
Else
    Grade ="A"
End If
```
End Function

Refer to Training File5.xls.

Scenario 12

Write a function to find a bonus based on grade (use Select Case). Grade bonus:

A 25000

B 20000

C 15000

D 10000

Refer to Training File5.xls.

Function bonus(grade)

```
Select Case grade

    Case "a", "A"
       bonus = 25000
    Case "b", "B"
       bonus = 20000
    Case "c", "C"
       bonus = 15000
    Case Else

       bonus = 10000

End Select
```

End Function

Scenario 13

Write a function to calculate DA based on region. DA is 5% if the region is either east or west, or else it will be 10%. Use the OR Operator to check multiple conditions.

OR Operator

The OR operator is used to perform a logical conjunction on two expressions. It returns true if any of the expression results are true.

Function CalcDa(Region, sal)
```
If Region = "east" Or Region = "west" Then
    CalcDa = sal * 0.05
Else


    CalcDa = sal * 0.1
EndIf
```
End Function

Scenario 14

Write a function to calculate DA based on region. DA is 5% if the region is east and salary is >10000. Otherwise, it is 10%.

Use the AND Operator to check multiple conditions.

AND Operator

This operator is used to perform a logical conjunction on two expressions. The AND operator returns true if all the expressions result in true.

Function CalcDa(Region, sal)
```
If Region = "east" And sal > 10000 Then
CalcDa = sal * 0.05
Else
CalcDa = sal * 0.1
EndIf
```

CONCLUSION

Functions and Subroutines are powerful tools in VBA that help you automate tasks and perform calculations in Excel. By understanding how to write procedures, use the Visual Basic Editor, and apply branching techniques, you can enhance your VBA programming skills and create more efficient and dynamic Excel applications.

EXERCISES

1. Write a Function to calculate the area of a rectangle given its length and width.

2. Create a Subroutine to format a range of cells based on specific conditions, such as highlighting cells with values above a certain threshold.

3. Develop a Function that converts a temperature from Fahrenheit to Celsius.

4. Write a Subroutine to sort a column of data in ascending order.

5. Create a Function to calculate the factorial of a given number.

CHAPTER 17

CONDITIONAL STATEMENTS IN VBA

INTRODUCTION

In Visual Basic for Applications (VBA), conditional statements are used to make decisions in your code based on certain conditions. They allow you to execute different blocks of code depending on the outcome of a logical expression. In this chapter, we will focus on two commonly used conditional statements in VBA: Select Case and If...End If.

STRUCTURE

In this chapter, we will go over the following topics:

- If...End If
- Select Case
- Select Case vs. If...End If

OBJECTIVES

By the end of this chapter, the reader will learn the differences between Select Case and If...End If statements in VBA and learn their appropriate usage in different scenarios.

IF...END IF

In VBA, the If...End If statement is used to evaluate a condition and execute a block of code if the condition is true. It can also be combined with ElseIf and Else clauses to handle multiple conditions. Here is an example of the basic syntax for the If...End If statement:

```
If condition1 Then

    ' Code block to execute if condition1 is True
ElseIf condition2 Then
    ' Code block to execute if condition2 is True and
    condition1 is False
Else

    ' Code block to execute if none of the previous conditions are
True

End If
```

The "condition" and "condition2" expressions in the above example are Boolean expressions that evaluate to either true or false.

It is important to note that the "If...End If statement can be nested within other control structures, like loops, and can be used in combination with other statements and keywords to create more complex logic in your VBA code.

EXAMPLE

If the score is equal to or greater than 90, it displays "Grade: A." If it is between 80 and 89, it displays "Grade: B," and so on. If the score does not meet any of the specified conditions, it displays "Grade: F."

```
Sub GradeEvaluation()
    Dim score As Integer

    ' Prompt the user to enter a score score = InputBox("Enter
    the score:")
```

```
' Evaluate the score and provide a corresponding grade If
score >= 90 Then
    MsgBox "Grade: A"
ElseIf score >= 80 Then
    MsgBox "Grade: B"
ElseIf score >= 70 Then
    MsgBox "Grade: C"
ElseIf score >= 60 Then
    MsgBox "Grade: D"

Else

    MsgBox "Grade: F"
End If
End Sub
```

SELECT CASE

The Select Case statement in VBA provides a concise and structured way to handle multiple conditions and execute different code blocks based on the value of a single expression. Here is a comprehensive explanation of its syntax and usage:

```
Select Case expression
    Case value1
        ' Code to execute if expression matches value1
    Case value2
        ' Code to execute if expression matches value2
    Case Else
        ' Code to execute if expression does not match any
        previous cases
End Select
```

Example

In this example, the program prompts the user to enter a fruit name. The Select Case statement then evaluates the input and displays a corresponding message based on the selected fruit. If the fruit is "apple," it displays a message about it being a healthy choice. If it is "banana," it mentions the potassium content. If it is "orange" or "mandarin," it highlights the citrus goodness. For any other input, it displays a generic message.

```
Sub FruitSelection()

    Dim fruit As String


    ' Prompt the user to enter a fruit name fruit =
    InputBox("Enter a fruit name:")
    ' Evaluate the fruit name and display corresponding
    message Select Case fruit
        Case "apple"
            MsgBox "You selected an apple. It's a healthy
            choice!"
        Case "banana"
            MsgBox "You selected a banana. It's a great source
            of potassium."
        Case "orange", "mandarin"
            MsgBox "You selected an orange or a mandarin. Enjoy
            the citrus goodness!"
        Case Else
            MsgBox "That's an interesting choice!"
    End Select
End Sub
```

SELECT CASE VS. IF ... END IF

Use the Select Case statement as an alternative to using ElseIf in If...Then...Else statements when comparing one expression to several different values.

While If...Then...Else statements can evaluate a different expression for each ElseIf statement, the Select Case statement evaluates an expression only once, at the top of the control structure.

CONCLUSION

In this chapter, we explored the differences between Select Case and If...End If statements in VBA. We learned that Select Case is a useful alternative when you have multiple conditions to evaluate against a single expression. It simplifies your code and improves readability. When you have distinct and unrelated conditions to consider, If...End If statements are more appropriate.

EXERCISES

1. Write a VBA program that asks the user to enter a day of the week (as a number from one to seven), then displays the corresponding day name. Use both Select Case and If...End If statements to implement the program.

2. Write a VBA program that asks the user to enter a number and determines if it is positive, negative, or zero. Use both Select Case and If...End If statements to implement the program.

CHAPTER 18

VARIABLES AND DATA TYPES IN VBA

INTRODUCTION

In this chapter, we will explore the fundamentals of variables and data types in VBA (Visual Basic for Applications). Variables are essential elements in programming that store and manipulate data during program execution, while data types define the nature of the data stored in variables. Understanding variables and data types is crucial for writing efficient and effective VBA code. We will cover topics such as declaring variables and constants, specifying data types, working with message boxes and input boxes, selecting cells, rows, and columns, and working with sheets, workbooks, and the application object.

STRUCTURE

In this chapter, we will cover the following topics:

- Variables and constants
- Declaring variables and constants
- Data types of variables and constants
- The message box and the input box
- Selecting and activating cells
- Selecting and activating rows and columns
- Working with Sheets
- Working with the Workbook
- Working with the application object

OBJECTIVES

By the end of the chapter, the reader will be able to understand the concept of variables and constants in VBA and how to declare them, be familiar with different data types available in VBA and their respective ranges and understand the usage of message boxes and input boxes for user interaction. Additionally, the reader will also learn techniques for selecting and activating cells, rows, and columns in Excel, and gain knowledge on working with sheets, workbooks, and the application object in VBA.

VARIABLES AND CONSTANTS

Let us now learn about variables and constants.

Variables

The features of variables are as follows:

- A variable is a named storage location containing data that can be modified during program execution.
- Each variable has a name that uniquely identifies it within its scope.
- A data type can be specified or not.
- Variable names:
  - Must begin with an alphabetic character,
  - Must be unique within the same scope,
  - Cannot be longer than 255 characters, and
  - Must contain an embedded period or type-declaration character.

Constant

A constant is a named item that retains a constant value throughout the execution of a program. A constant can be a string or a numeric literal.

DECLARING VARIABLES AND CONSTANTS

The syntax to declare a variable is:

DIM name_of_variable AS type_of_variable

For example:

Dim strName As String

Dim intX As Integer

Dim intX , intYAs Integer

The syntax to declare a constant is:

Const name_of_variable AS type_of_variable = constant value

For example, Const conAge As Integer = 34.

When declaring variables, use a Dim statement. For constants, use a Const statement.

A declaration statement can be placed within a procedure to create a procedure-level variable. It may also be placed at the top of a module, in the Declarations section, to create a module-level variable.

DATA TYPES OF VARIABLES AND CONSTANTS

Table 18.1 shows the various ranges in data type.

TABLE 18.1 Data Types

Data type	Range
Byte	0 to 255.
Integer	– 32,768 to 32,767.
Long	– 2,147,483,648 to 2,147,483,647.
Single	– 3.402823E38 to – 1.401298E – 45 (negative values).
	1.401298E – 45 to 3.402823E38 (positive values).
Double	– 1.7200369313486231E308 to
	– 4.94065645841247E – 324 (negative values). 4.94065645841247E – 324 to 1.7200369313486231E308
	(positive values).
Currency	– 922,337,203,685,477.5808 to 922,337,203,685,477.5807.
String	Zero to approximately two billion characters.
Variant	Date values: January 1, 100 to December 31, 9999.
	Numeric values: same range as Double.
	String values: same range as String.
	Can also contain Error or Null values.
Boolean	True or False.
Date	January 1, 100 to December 31, 9999.
Object	Any object reference.

Using the Option Explicit Statement

Use Option Explicit to enforce explicit declaration of variables. It must appear in a module before any procedure. If not used, undeclared variables will be of Variant type.

MESSAGE BOX AND INPUT BOX

The Msgbox function displays a message in a dialog box, waits for the user to click a button, and returns an Integer indicating which button the user clicked.

The InputBox Function displays a prompt in a dialog box, waits for the user to input text or click a button, and returns a string containing the contents of the text box.

Example:

Sub Greet()

```
    MsgBox "Hello " & InputBOx("What is your name?")
```
End Sub

SELECTING AND ACTIVATING CELLS

When you work with Microsoft Excel, you usually select a cell or cells and then perform an action, such as formatting the cells or entering values in them.

Refer to *Table 18.2* to write the codes for various actions.

TABLE 18.2 Codes for Various Actions

To do this	Write this code
Select cell A1	**Range("A1").select or Cells(1,1). select**
Select range A1:B5	**Range("A1:b5").select**
Select range A1:A5 and C2:C10	**Range("A1:A5 , C2:C10").select**
Select current cell	**Activecell.select**
Select range from current cell to B6	**Range(Activecell , "B6").select**
Select current region of activecell	**Activecell.currentregion.select**
Ctrl + Shift+ Down Arrow from Activecell	**Range(ActivecellActivecell.End(X lDown)).select**
Ctrl + Shift + Down Arrow from cell A2	**Range("A2" , Activecell.End(XlDown)). Select**

SELECTING AND ACTIVATING ROWS AND COLUMNS

Sometimes you need to select specific rows and columns and then perform actions.

To do this, write the code shown in the following *Table 18.3*.

TABLE 18.3 Codes for Various Actions

To do this	Write this code
Select a row	**Rows("2:2").select**
Select rows from 2 to 5	**Rows("2:5").select**
Select 3 rows from activecell	**Activecell.entirerow.Range("1:3"). select**
Select a column	**Columns("A:A").select**
Select columns from B to E	**Columns("B:E").select**
Select 3 columns from activecell	**Activecell.entirecolumn.Range("A:C").select**
Select current row	**Activecell.entirerow.select**
Select current column	**Activecell.entirecolumn.select**

WORKING WITH SHEETS

You will frequently need to select a specific sheet, insert a new sheet, rename a sheet, and so on. Refer to *Table 18.4*.

TABLE 18.4 Codes for Various Actions

To do This	Write This code
Select any sheet by index number	**Sheets(2).selectWorksheets(2) .select**
Select any sheet by name	**Sheets("Sheet1"). selectWorksheets("Sheet1").select**
Renaming a sheet	**Sheets("Sheet1").name="newname"**
Assign a new name	**Worksheets("Sheet1").name= Activesheet.name**
Delete a sheet	**Sheets("Sheet1").delete Worksheets("Sheet1").delete Activesheet.delete**
Insert a sheet	**Sheets.add before:= sheets("Sheet1") Worksheets.add before:=sheets("Sheet1")**

WORKING WITH A WORKBOOK

Sometimes you need to work with different workbooks. Refer to *Table 18.5*.

TABLE 18.5 Codes for Various Actions

To do This	Write this code
Open a workbook	**Workbooks.open filename:="filename with path"**
Open workbook which contains auto macros	**Workbooks. openfilename: =" Activeworkbook. runautomacros"**
Close a workbook	**Workbooks(2).close**
Add a new workbook	**Workbooks.add**

WORKING WITH THE APPLICATION OBJECT

Sometimes you will need to ignore some Excel messages. To do this, you need to work with the application object, as illustrated in *Table 18.6*.

TABLE 18.6 Codes for Various Actions

To do this	Write This Code
To switch off the display of messages	**Application.DisplayAlert = False**
To stop flickering of the screen	**Application.ScreenUpdating = False**
To stop copy / cut mode	**Application.CutCopyMode = False**
To calculate	**Application.Calculate**

Scenario 15

Create a macro which should accept the Name and City of a person and store it in an Excel worksheet in cell A1 and B1. If the user types Mumbai as the city, the font color must be red. Use the InputBox function to take input from the user. Use the MsgBox function to display results.

```
Sub Accept_Details()
Dim e_Name , e_City As String


Name = InputBox("Enter your name")
City = InputBox("Enter your city")
```

```
MsgBox "Your name is " & Name & " and city is " & City
Cells(1, 1).Value = e_Name Cells(1, 2).Value = e_City
If Cells(1, 2).Value = "mumbai" Then
     Cells(1, 2).Font.ColorIndex = 3
Else
     Cells(1, 2).Font.ColorIndex = 0
EndIf
```
End Sub

Scenario 16

Create a macro and name it "Data_Entry". It must accept the employee code, name, hire date, and salary of a person. Insert the values in the "Database" worksheet. Every new record must be stored after the last record.

Sub Data_Entry()

```
Dim EmpCode As integer, Next_Row as integer

Dim EmpName As String

Dim doj As Date

Dim Salary As Currency

EmpCode = InputBox("Enter Employee Code")
EmpName = InputBox("Enter Employee Name")
doj = InputBox("enter Date of Joining mm/dd/yy")
Salary = InputBox("Enter Salary of Employee")
Range("a65536").select
Selection.end(xlup).select Next_Row= activecell.row+1

Cells(Next_Row, 1).Value = EmpCode Cells(Next_Row, 2).Value =
EmpNameCells(Next_Row, 3).Value = Format(doj, "MMM DD YYYY")
Cells(Next_Row, 4).Value = Salary
```
End Sub

CONCLUSION

In conclusion, this chapter provided a comprehensive overview of variables and data types in VBA. It covered the declaration of variables and constants, explained different data types and their ranges, demonstrated the usage of message boxes and input boxes, and explored techniques for selecting and manipulating cells, rows, and columns in Excel. The chapter also touched upon working with sheets, workbooks, and the application object. By understanding these fundamentals, readers can write efficient and effective VBA code.

EXERCISE

1. Write a VBA macro that prompts the user to enter their name, age, and favorite color using input boxes. The macro should store the values in cells A1, B1, and C1 of the active worksheet. Additionally, if the user's age is greater than or equal to 18, the font color of the corresponding cell should be set to their favorite color. Test the macro by running it and entering different values.

19

Looping Structures in VBA

INTRODUCTION

In this chapter, we will delve into the topic of looping structures in Visual Basic for Applications (VBA). Loops are powerful tools that enable the repetitive execution of code, improving efficiency and automating tasks. This chapter explores different types of loops, such as Do...Loop, For...Next, and For Each...Next loops, as well as auto-executed macros that run based on specific events.

STRUCTURE

In this chapter, we will go over the following topics:

- Using Loops (repeating actions)
- Using Do...Loop statements
- Using For...Next statements
- Using For Each...Next statements
- Auto-Executed Macros

OBJECTIVES

By the end of this chapter, the reader will learn looping structures in VBA, such as Do...Loop, For...Next, and For Each...Next. The chapter also covers practical examples for their implementation.

USING LOOPS (REPEATING ACTION)

Looping allows you to run a group of statements repeatedly. Some loops repeat statements until a condition is False; others repeat statements until a condition is True. There are also loops that repeat statements a specific number of times or for each object in a collection.

Choosing a Loop to Use

There are various loops you can use, such as:

- *Do...Loop*: Looping while or until a condition is True.
- *For...Next*: Using a counter to run statements a specified number of times.
- *For Each...Next*: Repeating a group of statements for each object in a collection.

USING DO...LOOP STATEMENTS

You can use Do...Loop statements to run a block of statements an indefinite number of times. The statements are repeated either while a condition is True or until a condition becomes True.

Syntax:

```
Do [{While | Until} condition]
[statements]
[Exit Do]
[statements]
Loop
```

Repeating Statements While a Condition is True

In a Do...Loop statement there are two ways to use the While keyword to check a condition. You can check the condition before you enter the loop, or you can check it after the loop has run at least once.

Checking Condition Before You Enter the Loop

The syntax for checking the condition before you enter the loop is:

```
DO WHILE (condition)

    Code to be repeated

LOOP
```

Checking Condition After the Loop Has Run at Least Once

The syntax for checking the condition after the loop has run at least once is:

```
DO

    Code to be repeated

LOOP WHILE (condition)
```

Scenario 17

Write code to accept and validate a username. A blank name should not be allowed. Refer to Training File5.xls.

Refer to *Figure 19.1*.

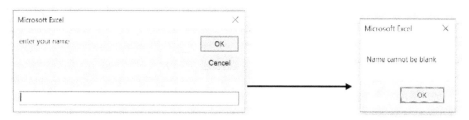

FIGURE 19.1 Scenario 17

```
Sub validate_name()
Dim name As String


name = InputBox("enter your name")
    Do While Trim(name) = ""
        MsgBox "Name cannot be blank"


        name = InputBox("enter your name")
    Loop
End Sub
```

NOTE *Trim function removes spaces from the beginning and end of the word.*

USING FOR...NEXT STATEMENTS

- You can use For...Next statements to repeat a block of statements a specific number of times.
- The For loop uses a counter variable whose value is increased or decreased with each internal repetition of the loop.

Syntax:

```
FOR counter_variable = initial_value TO Final_Value
STEPstep_value Code to be repeated
NEXT
```

NOTE *The smaller the data type, the less time it takes to update.*

Scenario 18

Create a macro named "fill_series" to display numbers from one to ten (starting with cell A1).

Sub fill_series()

```
Dim fill_val As Integer
Range("A1").Select For
fill_val = 1 To 10
```

```
ActiveCell.Value = fill_val
ActiveCell.Offset(1, 0).Select Next
```

End Sub

Offset function() is used to point to or refer to the object up, down, left, or right of the object.

Syntax:

OFFSET(row , column) Example

1. Activecell.Offset(1,0).select: This will select the cell 1 row down and 0 column to the right of the Activecell.

2. Activecell.Offset(0,1).select: This will select the cell 0 row down and 1 column to the right of the Activecell.

3. Activecell.Offset(-1,0).select: This will select the cell 1 row up and 0 column to the right of the Activecell.

4. Activecell.Offset(0,-1).select: This will select the cell 0 row down and 1 column to the left of the Activecell.

USING FOR EACH... NEXT STATEMENTS

For Each...Next statements repeat a block of statements for each object in a collection or element in an array.

Visual Basic automatically sets a variable each time the loop runs.

Any number of Exit For statements may be placed anywhere in the loop as an alternative way to exit.

Syntax:

For Each *element* In *group*

```
[statements]
[Exit For]
[statements]
Next [element]
```

Required: Variable used to iterate through the elements of the collection or array. For collections, *element* can only be a Variant variable, a generic object variable, or any specific object variable. For arrays, *element* can only be a Variant variable.

Group: Required. The name of an object collection or array

Statements

Optional. One or more statements that are executed on each item in *group*.

Scenario 19

Create a macro titled "UPPER_CASE" to convert data into capital letters. Use the Ucase () function to convert the case into capital letters.

Refer to *Figure 19.2*.

BEFORE

	A	B	C
1	Empcod	First Nam	Last Nam
2	1	Raja	Raymondeka
3	2	Kuldeep	Sharma
4	2	Suman	Shinde
5	3	Beena	Mavadia
6	4	Seema	Ranganathan
7	5	Deepak	Jain
8	5	Julie	D'Souza
9	6	Neena	Mukherjee
10	7	Pankaj	Sutradhar
11	8	Andre	Fernendes
12	9	Sujay	Madhrani
13	10	Shilpa	Lele
14	11	Meera	Lalwani
15	7	Sheetal	Desai

AFTER

	A	B	C
1	Empcod	First Nam	Last Nam
2	1	RAJA	Raymondeka
3	2	KULDEEP	Sharma
4	2	SUMAN	Shinde
5	3	BEENA	Mavadia
6	4	SEEMA	Ranganathan
7	5	DEEPAK	Jain
8	5	JULIE	D'Souza
9	6	NEENA	Mukherjee
10	7	PANKAJ	Sutradhar
11	8	ANDRE	Fernendes
12	9	SUJAY	Madhrani
13	10	SHILPA	Lele
14	11	MEERA	Lalwani
15	7	SHEETAL	Desai

FIGURE 19.2 Scenario 19

```
Sub UPPER_CASE()

    Dim wscell As Range
    For Each wscell In Selection
        wscell.Value = UCase(wscell.Value)
    Next
End Sub
```

Scenario 20

Create a macro named "lower_case" to convert data into small letters. Use the lcase () function to convert the case into lowercase letters.

Refer to *Figure 19.3*.

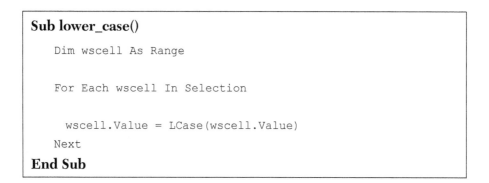

FIGURE 19.3 Scenario 20

```
Sub lower_case()

    Dim wscell As Range


    For Each wscell In Selection


      wscell.Value = LCase(wscell.Value)

    Next
End Sub
```

Scenario 21

Create a macro titled "Proper_case" to convert data into title case letters. Use the WorksheetFunction object to use any function from Excel in VBA. Refer to *Figure 19.4*.

BEFORE		AFTER	

	A	B	C
1	Empcod	First Nan	Last Nan
2	1	raja	Raymondeka
3	2	kuldeep	Sharma
4	2	suman	Shinde
5	3	beena	Mavadia
6	4	seema	Ranganathan
7	5	deepak	Jain
8	5	julie	D'Souza
9	6	neena	Mukherjee
10	7	pankaj	Sutradhar
11	8	andre	Fernendes
12	9	sujay	Madhrani
13	10	shilpa	Lele

	A	B	C
1	Empcod	First Nan	Last Nan
2	1	Raja	Raymondeka
3	2	Kuldeep	Sharma
4	2	Suman	Shinde
5	3	Beena	Mavadia
6	4	Seema	Ranganathan
7	5	Deepak	Jain
8	5	Julie	D'Souza
9	6	Neena	Mukherjee
10	7	Pankaj	Sutradhar
11	8	Andre	Fernendes
12	9	Sujay	Madhrani
13	10	Shilpa	Lele
14	11	Meera	Lalwani
15	7	Sheetal	Desai

FIGURE 19.4 Scenario 21

```
Sub Proper_Case()

Dim wscell As Range

For Each wscell In Selection

    wscell.Value = Application.WorksheetFunction.
    Proper(wscell.Value)
Next
End Sub
```

Scenario 22

Open Scenario 22 and modify it. After storing the recorded macro, you should ask the user whether or not to continue and run per the user response. If the user clicks OK, it should continue the data entry. If the user clicks on Cancel, it should display "Thanks" and end the macro. Refer to *Figure 19.5*.

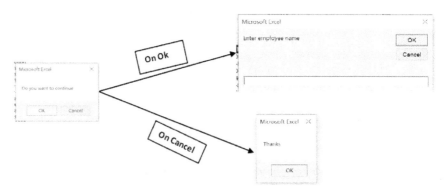

FIGURE 19.5 Scenario 22

```
Sub Data_Entry1()

    Dim EmpCode As Integer, next_row As Integer
    Dim EmpName As String
    Dim doj As Date
    Dim Salary As Currency


    Worksheets("database").Select
    Range("a65536").Select
    Selection.End(xlUp).Select
    next_row = ActiveCell.Row + 1


    Do
      EmpCode = InputBox("Enter Employee Code")
      EmpName = InputBox("Enter Employee Name")
      doj = InputBox("enter Date of Joining mm/dd/yy")
      Salary = InputBox("Enter Salary of Employee")
      Cells(next_row , 1).Value = EmpCode
      Cells(next_row , 2).Value = EmpName
      Cells(next_row , 3).Value = Format(doj, "MMM DD YYYY")
      Cells(next_row , 4).Value = Salary
      next_row =next_row + 1
    Loop While (MsgBox("Do you want to continue?", vbOKCancel)
    = vbOK)
    MsgBox "Thanks"
End Sub
```

Scenario 23

Create a macro which will calculate the following for each employee:

- HRA (75% of the salary)
- DA (60% of the salary)
- TOTAL (salary + HRA + DA)

Refer to *Figure 19.6*.

	A	B	C	D	E	F	G	H
1	Empcode	First Name	Last Name	Dept	Region	Deptcode	Hiredate	Salary
2	1	raja	Raymondeka	Sales	north	10	01-Jan-16	85000
3	2	kuldeep	Sharma	Admin	north	70	01-Mar-17	40000
4	2	suman	Shinde	Sales	south	10	01-Jan-10	60000
5	3	beena	Mavadia	Mktg	east	20	24-Nov-12	30000
6	4	seema	Ranganathan	R&D	north	30	04-Sep-13	80000
7	5	deepak	Jain	Personal	east	60	17-Aug-04	39000
8	5	julie	D'Souza	R&D	west	30	04-Sep-06	31000
9	6	neena	Mukherjee	R&D	north	30	04-Sep-08	31000
10	7	pankaj	Sutradhar	Sales	north	10	05-Sep-08	45000
11	8	andre	Fernendes	Mktg	north	20	06-Sep-08	50000
12	9	sujay	Madhvani	Finance	east	40	07-Sep-08	45000
13	10	shilpa	Lele	Admin	west	70	01-Mar-90	80000

	A	B	C	D	E	F	G	H	I	J	K
1	Empcode	First Name	Last Name	Dept	Region	Deptcode	Hiredate	Salary	DA	HRA	Gross
2	1	raja	Raymondeka	Sales	north	10	01-Jan-16	85000	51,000.00	63,750.00	1,99,750.00
3	2	kuldeep	Sharma	Admin	north	70	01-Mar-17	40000	24,000.00	30,000.00	94,000.00
4	2	suman	Shinde	Sales	south	10	01-Jan-10	60000	36,000.00	45,000.00	1,41,000.00
5	3	beena	Mavadia	Mktg	east	20	24-Nov-12	30000	18,000.00	22,500.00	70,500.00
6	4	seema	Ranganathan	R&D	north	30	04-Sep-13	80000	48,000.00	60,000.00	1,88,000.00
7	5	deepak	Jain	Personal	east	60	17-Aug-04	39000	23,400.00	29,250.00	91,650.00
8	5	julie	D'Souza	R&D	west	30	04-Sep-06	31000	18,600.00	23,250.00	72,850.00
9	6	neena	Mukherjee	R&D	north	30	04-Sep-08	31000	18,600.00	23,250.00	72,850.00
10	7	pankaj	Sutradhar	Sales	north	10	05-Sep-08	45000	27,000.00	33,750.00	1,05,750.00
11	8	andre	Fernendes	Mktg	north	20	06-Sep-08	50000	30,000.00	37,500.00	1,17,500.00
12	9	sujay	Madhvani	Finance	east	40	07-Sep-08	45000	27,000.00	33,750.00	1,05,750.00
13	10	shilpa	Lele	Admin	west	70	01-Mar-90	80000	48,000.00	60,000.00	1,88,000.00

FIGURE 19.6 Scenario 23

There could be two ways to solve this question.

Refer to Training File6.xls.

1. Through a macro, you can put formulae into the cells:

```
Sub Gross_Salary()
'The user will select the range H2:H101 cells As Range.
For Each wscell In Selection
    wscell.Offset(0, 1).Value = "=rc[-1]*75%"
    wscell.Offset(0, 2).Value = "=rc[-2]*60%"
    wscell.Offset(0, 3).Value = "=sum(rc[-1]:rc[-3])"
Next
End Sub
```

2. Calculate using your macro and put only the results in the cells:

Sub Gross_Salary()

```
User will select the range H2:H101 Dim wscell As Range


For Each wscell In Selection


    wscell.Offset(0, 1).Value= wscell.Value * .75
    wscell.Offset(0, 2).Value = wscell.Value * 60%
    wscell.Offset(0, 3).Value = wscell.value + wscell.Offset(0,
    1).Value + wscell.Offset(0, 2).Value
Next
```

End Sub

Scenario 24

Create a macro to display a list of names of worksheets in the current workbook. Refer to Figure 19.7.

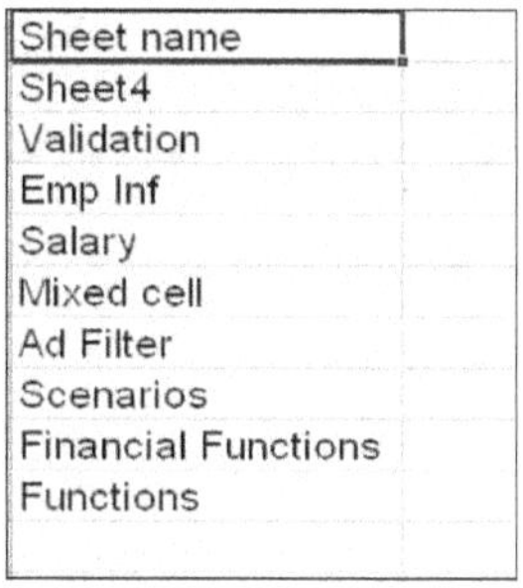

Sheet name
Sheet4
Validation
Emp Inf
Salary
Mixed cell
Ad Filter
Scenarios
Financial Functions
Functions

FIGURE 19.7 Scenario 24

Sub list_sheets()

```
„ Declare a variable as worksheet object
Dim sht As Worksheet
    For Each sht In Worksheets
        ActiveCell.Value = sht.name
        ActiveCell.Offset(1, 0).Select
Next
```

End Sub

AUTO-EXECUTED MACROS

The syntax is:

```
fydyr
```

Refer to *Table 19.1.*

TABLE 19.1 Auto-Executed Macros

To	Use
Run a macro as soon as the workbook gets opened	**Sub auto_open()** **End Sub**
Run a macro as soon as the workbook is closed	**Sub auto_close()** **End Sub**

Practice 3

```
Function Search_sheet(newSht)
    Dim sht As Worksheet
For Each sht In Worksheets
    If UCase(sht.name) = UCase(newSht) Then
        Search_sheet = "Sheet(" & newSht & ") exists"
        Exit Function
     End If
    Next
    Search_sheet = "Sheet(" & newSht & ") does not exists"
End Function
```

Write a function ("Search_sheet") to check for the existence of any sheet.

Practice 4

Write a macro to increase the salary by 2000 for each employee.

Scenario 25

Create a macro to generate a region-based and department-based sum of the salary and count of employees using a pivot table. Modify the code in such a way that each pivot should be generated from current data.

Sub Pivot_Summary()

```
Range("A2").Select
ActiveWorkbook.PivotCaches.Add(SourceType:=xlDatabase,
SourceData:=
_ Range("a2").CurrentRegion).CreatePivotTable
TableDestination:="",
TableName:= _ "PivotTable2",
DefaultVersion:=xlPivotTableVersion10


ActiveSheet.PivotTableWizard TableDestination:=ActiveSheet.
Cells(3, 1)
ActiveSheet.Cells(3, 1).Select
ActiveSheet.PivotTables("PivotTable2").AddFields
RowFields:=Array("Region", _ "Dept", "Data")


With ActiveSheet.PivotTables("PivotTable2").
PivotFields("salary")
    .Orientation = xlDataField
    .Position = 1
End With

With ActiveSheet.PivotTables("PivotTable2").
PivotFields("Empcode")
    .Orientation = xlDataField
    .Caption = "Count of Empcode"
    .Function = xlCount
End With
Range("C3").Select

With ActiveSheet.PivotTables("PivotTable2").DataPivotField
    .Orientation = xlColumnField
    .Position = 1
End With
```
End Sub

Refer to Training File6.xls.

Scenario 26

Write a code to remove duplicate records from the "daily" worksheet if they exist in the "master" worksheet. (Use a nested loop.)

Solution 26

Refer to Training File7.xls.

```
Sub duplicates()


Dim wscell As Range, tcell As Range
Worksheets("master").Select
Range("a2").Select
Range(ActiveCell, ActiveCell.End(xlDown)).Select
For Each wscell In Selection
    Worksheets("daily").Select
    Range("a2").Select
Range(ActiveCell, ActiveCell.End(xlDown)).Select
For Each tcell In Selection
    If tcell.Value = wscell.Value Then
    tcell.EntireRow.Delete End If
  Next
Next
ActiveCell.Select
End Sub
```

The same code can be written using the find command, as shown.

```
Sub duplicates_With_find()
    Worksheets("master").Select
        Rangec("a2").Select
        Range(ActiveCell, ActiveCell.End(xlDown)).Select
        For Each tcell In Selection
            Worksheets("daily").Select
            Set c = Cells.Find(What:=tcell.Value)
            If Not c Is Nothing Then Rows(c.Row).Delete
            End If
    Next
End Sub
```

Scenario 27

Create a macro named "Merging_Sheets" which will copy data from all worksheets into one worksheet.

Your macro should generate a pivot for the total of the quantity sold per region, and then for the emp code after consolidation.

Solution

Sub Merging_Sheets()

```
Scenario27
'Add a sheet at the end and name it as consolidate and create
    headings
Worksheets.Add After:=Worksheets(Worksheets.Count)
ActiveSheet.Name = "consolidate"
ActiveSheet.Range("a1").Select
Range("a1").Value = "Product"
Range("b1").Value = "Sales"
Copy data from every worksheet to consolidate worksheet
For Index = 1 To Worksheets.Count - 1
    Worksheets(Index).Select
    Range("a2").Select
    Range(Selection, Selection.End(xlDown)).Select
    Range(Selection, Selection.End(xlToRight)).Select
    Selection.Copy
    Worksheets("consolidate").Select
Cells(Range("a65536").End(xlUp).Row + 1, 1).Select
ActiveSheet.Paste
Next, generate a pivot on consolidated data.
Sheets("consolidate").Select Range("A1").Select
    Application.CutCopyMode = False
    ActiveWorkbook.PivotCaches.Add(SourceType:=xlDatabase,
SourceData:= _
        Range("a1").CurrentRegion).CreatePivotTable
TableDestination:="", TableName _
```

```
        :="PivotTable1", DefaultVersion:=xlPivotTableVersion10
ActiveSheet.PivotTableWizard TableDestination:=ActiveSheet.
Cells(3, 1) ActiveSheet.Cells(3, 1).Select ActiveSheet.
PivotTables("PivotTable1").AddFields RowFields:="Product"
ActiveSheet.PivotTables("PivotTable1").PivotFields("Sales").
Orientation = _ xlDataField
```
End Sub

CONCLUSION

Mastering looping structures is essential for effective VBA programming. By utilizing loops, you can automate repetitive tasks, process large amounts of data, and enhance the overall efficiency of your VBA programs. This chapter provides a comprehensive overview of loops and their applications in VBA, equipping you with the skills to write concise and powerful code that saves time and effort.

EXERCISES

1. Write a VBA macro named "PrintNumbers" that prints numbers from 1 to 100 in the Immediate Window.

2. Create a VBA macro named "CalculateSum" that calculates the sum of numbers from 1 to 10 and displays the result in a message box.

3. Write a VBA macro named "EvenNumbers" that prints all even numbers from 1 to 20 in the Immediate Window.

4. Create a VBA macro named "Factorial" that calculates the factorial of a given number. The macro should prompt the user to enter a number, then display the factorial result in a message box.

5. Write a VBA macro named "ReverseString" that prompts the user to enter a string, then prints the reverse of the string in the Immediate Window.

6. Create a VBA macro named "TableOfSquares" that generates a table of squares from 1 to 10. The macro should display the number and its square in separate columns in a new worksheet.

7. Write a VBA macro named "CountCharacters" that counts the number of characters in a given string. The macro should prompt the user to enter a string, then display the count in a message box.

20

ARRAYS AND COLLECTIONS IN VBA

INTRODUCTION

Arrays and Collections are essential components in VBA programming, enabling efficient storage and manipulation of multiple values. In this chapter, we will explore their concepts, learn how to declare and use them, understand array indexing and dynamic arrays, and examine practical examples of their application in VBA.

STRUCTURE

In this chapter, we will discuss the following topics:

- Arrays
- Declaring the Arrays
- Using Arrays
- Array Indexing
- Declaring a Dynamic Array
- Resizing a Dynamic Array

OBJECTIVES

By the end of this chapter, the reader will learn the purpose of arrays and collections in VBA programming, learn how to declare, resize, and use arrays efficiently, and understand the advantages of collections over arrays for advanced data manipulation tasks.

ARRAYS

Arrays are a set of sequentially indexed elements having the same intrinsic data type. Each element of an array has a unique identifying index number.

Changes made to one element of an array do not affect the other elements. The different types of arrays are as follows:

- An array whose size is specified is a fixed-size array.
- An array whose size can be changed while a program is running is a dynamic array.
- A single dimension array contains only rows.
- A multiple dimension array uses rows and columns.

DECLARING THE ARRAYS

Arrays are declared the same way as other variables.

Syntax:

Dim name_Of_array(Size) As Data_Type

Example

Single dimension: Declaring a single dimension array variable of row size 10, which can store integer items.

Dim Myarray(10) As Integer

Multiple dimension (Max 60 dimensions): Declaring a multiple dimension array variable of three rows and five columns, which can store 15 integer items.

Dim Myarray(3 , 5) As Integer

USING ARRAYS

Using arrays can be explained with an example. To store daily expenses for each day of the month, you can declare one array variable with 31 elements, rather than declaring 31 variables.

Each element in an array contains one value.

Sub Single_array()
```
Dim curExpense(31) As Currency
Dim intI As Integer
For intI = 0 to 31
    curExpense(intI) = 20
Next
```
End Sub

NOTE *In the above example, array index will start from zero.*

ARRAY INDEXING

All array indexes begin at zero. Whether an array is indexed from 0 or 1 depends on the setting of the Option Base statement.

If Option Base 1 is not specified, all array indexes begin at zero.

Example

Option Base 1
```
Sub Single_array()
Dim curExpense(31) As Currency
Dim intI As Integer
For intI = 1 to 31
    curExpense(intI) = 20
Next
```
End Sub

NOTE *In the above example, array index will start from one.*

DECLARING A DYNAMIC ARRAY

By declaring a dynamic array, you can size the array while the code is running. Use a Dim statement to declare an array, leaving the parentheses empty.

Syntax:

Dim Name_Of_Array() As Data_Type

RESIZING A DYNAMIC ARRAY

Use the ReDim statement to declare an array implicitly within a procedure.

Be careful not to misspell the name of the array when you use the ReDim statement.

Array Example

Option Base 1 ' Initializing the array index 1

```
Sub Searchdata()
Dim mycell_array() As String ' Declaring the dynamic array
Dim a, i As Long
i = 1
Sheets(1).Select
    a = Range("a65536").End(xlUp).Row - 1
    ReDim mycell_array(a) ' Redeclaring the array size
    Range("a2", Range("a2").End(xlDown)).Select
    For Each mycell In Selection mycell_array(i) = mycell i
        = i + 1
    Next
Sheets("database").Select
Range("a2", Range("a2").End(xlDown)).Select
i = 1
For i = 1 To a
    For Each mycell In Selection
        If mycell_array(i) = mycell Then
        mycell.EntireRow.Delete 'mycell.Offset(0, 1).Value =
        "found"
        End If
Next
```

End Sub

CONCLUSION

Arrays and Collections are powerful tools in VBA programming, facilitating the management of data sets and enhancing code efficiency. With a solid grasp of these concepts, you can optimize your VBA code, improve readability, and handle complex data structures effectively. Incorporating arrays and collections into your programming repertoire will expand your capabilities and enable you to tackle a wider range of VBA projects.

EXERCISES

1. Declare a dynamic array to store the daily expenses of five employees.

2. Use a loop to input the expenses for each employee for a specified number of days.

3. Calculate the total expenses for each employee and display the result.

4. Determine the employee with the highest total expenses and print their name and the corresponding amount.

5. Calculate the average expenses per day for the entire team and display the result.

CHAPTER 21

DEBUGGING AND ERROR HANDLING IN VBA

INTRODUCTION

In this chapter, we will explore the important concepts of debugging and error handling in Visual Basic for Applications (VBA). Debugging is the process of identifying and resolving runtime errors and logical errors in our VBA code. Error handling involves implementing strategies to handle and manage errors that occur during the execution of our code. By understanding these concepts and utilizing appropriate techniques, we can create more robust and reliable VBA macros.

STRUCTURE

In this chapter, we will go over the following topics:

- Errors
- Error Handling
- Error Numbers
- Debugging the Macro

OBJECTIVES

By the end of this chapter, the reader will learn about errors, error handling, and error numbers, which, along with debugging, are crucial in VBA.

ERRORS

An error is generated if a statement fails. There are three types of errors:

- *Logical*: When the macro does not give the expected result. These errors can be handled by a change in logic and the trial and error method
- *Technical*: A runtime failure of any statement. Use the On Error statement to handle these errors.
- *Syntax*: These include incorrectly spelled keywords, mismatched parentheses, and a wide variety of other errors. Excel will flag your syntax errors and prevent the code from executing until they are corrected.

ERROR HANDLING

There are three ways to handle errors:

- Whenever an error is encountered, direct the control to the specific label or line of code.
  - On Error GoTo line / label On Error
- Continue with the statement immediately following the statement that caused the run-time error.
  - On Error Resume Next
- Disable any enabled error handler in the current procedure.
  - On Error GoTo 0

NOTE *An error-handling routine is not a Sub procedure or a Function procedure. It is a section of code marked by a line label or line number. If you do not use an On Error statement, any runtime error that occurs is fatal; an error message is displayed and execution stops.*

Scenario 28

Open *Scenario 22*. It will generate an error if the Database worksheet does not exist. Modify the code to handle this error; your program should add a new worksheet if the Database worksheet does not exist.

NOTE *Use On Error GoTo line / label.*

Solution

Sub Error_handling1()

```vba
On Error GoTo err_handler
Dim EmpCode As Integer, next_row As Integer
Dim EmpName As String
Dim doj As Date

Dim Salary As Currency
Worksheets("database").Select
Range("a65536").Select
Selection.End(xlUp).Select
next_row = ActiveCell.Row + 1
Do

  EmpCode = InputBox("Enter Employee
  Code") EmpName = InputBox("Enter
  Employee Name")
  doj = InputBox("enter Date of Joining mm/dd/yy")
  Salary = InputBox("Enter Salary of Employee")
  Cells(next_row , 1).Value = EmpCode Cells(next_row ,
  2).Value = EmpName
  Cells(next_row , 3).Value = Format(doj, "MMM DD YYYY")
  Cells(next_row , 4).Value = Salary
  next_row =next_row + 1
Loop While (MsgBox("Do you want to continue?", vbOKCancel) =
  vbOK) MsgBox "Thanks"
  Exit Sub

  err_handler: Worksheets.Add
  ActiveSheet.name ="database"
  Range("a1").Value = "Emp Code"
  Range("b1").Value = "Emp Name"
  Range("c1").Value = "Date of Joining"
  Range("d1").Value = "Salary"
  Resume Next
```

End Sub

ERROR NUMBER

Each runtime error has a number. If you know the number, you can trap the error by its number. For example, refer to *Table 21.1*.

TABLE 21.1 Error Numbers and Their Descriptions

Error Number	Description
61	Disk Full
4	Application defined or Object defined error
7	Out of memory
9	Subscript out of range

Try the following code to see the error for a particular error number.

```
Sub Show_Error():

Dim ErrorNumber


  For ErrorNumber = 61 To 64 ' Loop through values 61 - 64.
     Msgbox Error(ErrorNumber)
  Next ErrorNumber


End Sub
```

Scenario 29

Open *Scenario 28*. If you leave inputbox empty, your macro will generate an error. Modify the code as follows (use On error resume next).

```
Sub Error_handling2()
  Dim EmpCode As Integer, next_row As Integer
  Dim EmpName As String
  Dim doj As Date
  Dim Salary As Currency
  ' If there is any error it should continue with the next line
On Error resume Next
```

```
    Worksheets("database").Select Range("a65536").Select
    Selection.End(xlUp).Select next_row
    = ActiveCell.Row + 1
Do
    EmpCode = InputBox("Enter Employee Code")
    EmpName = InputBox("Enter Employee Name")
    doj = InputBox("enter Date of Joining mm/dd/yy")
    Salary = InputBox("Enter Salary of Employee")
    Cells(next_row , 1).Value = EmpCode Cells(next_row , 2).
    Value =EmpName
    Cells(next_row , 3).Value = Format(doj, "MMM DD YYYY")
    Cells(next_row , 4).Value = Salary next_row =next_row + 1
    Loop While (MsgBox("Do you want to continue?", vbOKCancel)
    = vbOK) MsgBox "Thanks"
End Sub
```

DEBUGGING THE MACRO

Debugging is the process of finding and correcting runtime errors and logical errors. Press *F8* to execute code one line at a time.

The Debug toolbar can be seen in *Figure 21.1.*

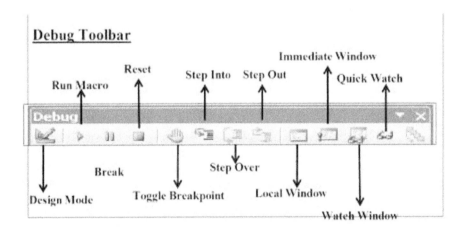

FIGURE 21.1 Debug Toolbar

Here are the various toolbar buttons:

- *Design Mode*: Turns design mode off and on.
- *Run Sub/UserForm or Run Macro*: Runs the current procedure if the cursor is in a procedure, runs the UserForm if a UserForm is currently active, or runs a macro if neither the Code window nor a UserForm is active.
- *Break*: Stops execution of a program while it is running and switches to break mode.
- *Reset*: Clears the execution stack and module level variables and resets the project.
- *Toggle Breakpoint*: Sets or removes a breakpoint at the current line.
- *Step Into*: Executes code one statement at a time.
- *Step Over*: Executes code one procedure or statement at a time in the Code window.
- *Step Out*: Executes the remaining lines of a procedure in which the current execution point lies.
- *Locals Window*: Displays the Locals window.
- *Immediate Window*: Displays the Immediate window.
- *Watch Window*: Displays the Watch window.
- *Quick Watch*: Displays the Quick Watch dialog box with the current value of the selected expression.
- *Call Stack*: Displays the Calls dialog box, which lists the currently active procedure calls (procedures in the application that have started but are not completed).

Here are some tips that will help you keep errors to a minimum:

- Use an Option Explicit. This will force you to define the data type for every variable that you use. This will avoid the common error of misspelling a variable name.
- Format your code with indentation. If you have several nested For...Next loops, consistent indentation will make it much easier to keep track of them all.
- Be careful with On Error Resume Next. This statement causes Excel to ignore any errors and continue. In some cases, using this statement will cause Excel to ignore errors that should not be ignored. You may have bugs and not even realize it.

- Use comments. Make a habit of writing comments, so that when you revisit your code you can understand the logic. Adding a few comments to describe your logic can save you significant time.
- Keep your subroutines and functions simple. Write your code in smaller modules, each of which has a single, well-defined purpose.
- Use the macro recorder to identify properties and methods. If you do not remember the name or syntax of a property or method, record a macro, and look at the recorded code.
- Consider a different approach. If you are having trouble getting a particular routine to work correctly, you might want to scrap the idea and try something completely different. In most cases, Excel offers several alternative methods of accomplishing the same thing.
- Use the debug toolbar.

CONCLUSION

Debugging and error handling are essential skills for VBA developers. By effectively managing errors and debugging our code, we can create more robust and error-free macros. Applying best practices, such as proper code formatting and commenting, and using the available debugging tools will help prevent and resolve errors efficiently.

EXERCISES

1. Open a new Excel workbook and navigate to the Visual Basic Editor (VBE).

2. In the VBE, insert a new module for writing the VBA code.

3. Create a subroutine named "CalculateStatistics" that takes no parameters.

4. Declare the necessary variables for storing input values and calculated statistics.

5. Implement error handling using advanced error handling techniques, such as "On Error GoTo," "On Error Resume Next," and "Err.Raise."

6. Prompt the user to input a range of numbers from the worksheet using the "Application.InputBox" method.

7. Use the "WorksheetFunction" object to perform the following calculations on the selected range:

   a. Calculate the sum of the numbers.

   b. Calculate the average of the numbers.

   c. Calculate the maximum value in the range.

   d. Calculate the minimum value in the range.

8. Display the calculated statistics in separate message boxes.

9. Include comprehensive error handling to handle scenarios such as invalid input, empty selection, non-numeric values in the range, or division by zero errors.

10. Test the macro by executing it with different inputs and verify that it handles errors effectively and provides accurate results.

CHAPTER 22

USER FORMS AND USER INPUT IN VBS

INTRODUCTION

User Forms and user input are essential aspects of creating interactive and user-friendly applications in Visual Basic Scripting (VBS). User Forms allow developers to design intuitive interfaces and capture user input for various purposes. By utilizing controls such as labels, text boxes, buttons, and more, VBS developers can create dynamic and responsive forms that enhance the overall user experience.

In this chapter, we will explore the process of creating User Forms in VBS, including designing the form layout, adding controls, and handling events. We will also discuss how to incorporate user input into your scripts, enabling your applications to respond to user actions and perform relevant tasks.

STRUCTURE

In this chapter, we will go over the following topics:

* User Forms
* Creating User forms
* Adding Other Controls
* Handling Events for the Control

OBJECTIVES

By the end of this chapter, the reader will learn about user forms and how to create them, add other controls, and handle events for the control. Understanding User Forms and user input in VBS will enable you to build interactive and functional applications that meet the specific needs of your users.

USER FORMS

User Forms can be used to create a customized Dialogue Box. Refer to *Figure 22.1.*

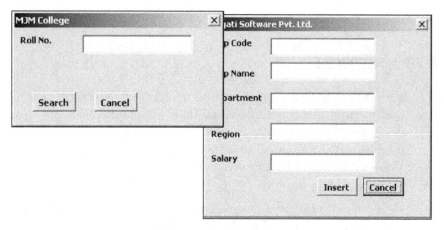

FIGURE 22.1 User Forms

CREATING USER FORMS

To create a user form, follow these steps:

1. Click Insert Menu.

2. Select UserForm, as shown in *Figure 22.2 (a)*.

3. This will add one object, UserForm1, in your workbook, as shown in *Figure 22.2 (b)*.

4. Use the Properties window to change the name, behavior, and appearance of the form. For example, to change the caption on a form, set the Caption property, as shown in *Figure 22.2 (c)*.

Refer to *Figure 22.2*.

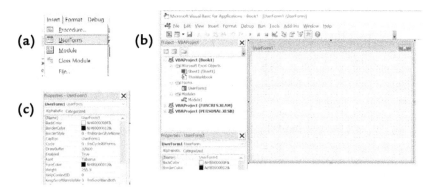

FIGURE 22.2 Creating User Forms

ADDING OTHER CONTROLS

To add other controls, follow these steps:

1. Click toolbox in toolbars, as shown in *Figure 22.3 (a)*.

2. Drag the control onto the form, as shown in *Figure 22.3 (b)*.

3. Change the properties, such as name, font, and so on, from the Property window, as shown in *Figure 22.3 (c)*.

Refer to *Figure 22.3*.

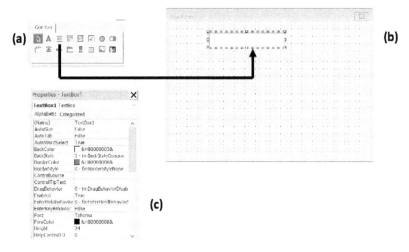

FIGURE 22.3 Adding Other Controls

HANDLING EVENTS FOR THE CONTROL

To handle events for the control, follow these steps:

1. Open the code window for the form.

2. Select the form control.

3. Click the View code tool from the project explorer window, as shown in *Figure 22.4 (a)*.

4. Select the control which you have placed in your form from *Figure 22.4 (b)*.

5. Select the event for your control, as shown in *Figure 22.4 (c)*.

6. Write code for the event, as shown in *Figure 22.4 (d)*.

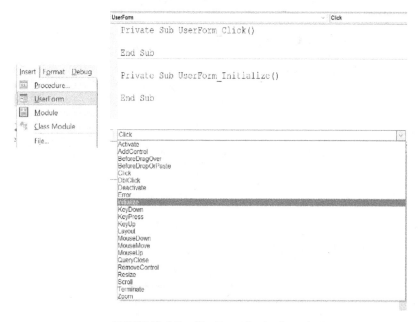

FIGURE 22.4 Handling Events for the Control

Scenario 30

Create a UserForm which will accept the participant's information to get enrolled for the training. The form should have Insert and Cancel command buttons. When the Insert button is clicked, the information entered in the form must go into Excel. When the Cancel button is clicked, the Form should be closed.

Solution

Follow the steps below.

1. Insert a UserForm.

2. Change the name and caption from the property window.

3. The name of the form should be "USR_enroll."

4. The caption should be "Training Enrollment Form."

5. Design the form as shown in *Figure 22.5.*

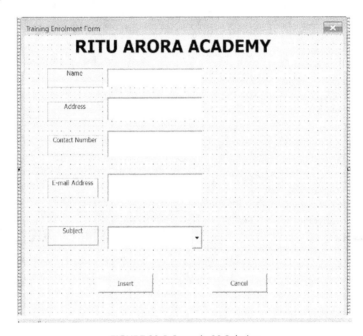

FIGURE 22.5 Scenario 30 Solution

This example has several properties.

- *Label*: Displays descriptive text.
- *TextBox*: A TextBox is the control most commonly used to display information entered by a user.
- *ListBox*: Displays a list of values and lets you select one or more.
- *ComboBox*: Combines the features of a ListBox and a TextBox. The user can enter a new value, as with a TextBox, or the user can select an existing value, as with a ListBox.

▦ *Frame*: Creates a functional and visual control group.

▦ *Properties*: Attributes (properties or variables).

▦ *Methods*: Operations the object will perform with the attribute.

Refer to the following *Table 22.1.*

TABLE 22.1 Employee UserForm

Control	Name	Property	Value
Label	**LBL_header**	Caption	Ritu Arora Academy
Label	**LBL_name**	Caption	Name
Label	**LBL_address**	Caption	Address
Label	**LBL_contactno**	Caption	Contact No.
Label	**LBL_email**	Caption	Email-id
Label	**LBL_Subject**	Caption	Subject
TextBox	**TXT_name**		
TextBox	**TXT_address**		
TextBox	**TXT_contactno**		
TextBox	**TXT_email**		
TextBox	**TXT_companyname**	Text	Enter your company name
Frame	**FRM_details**	Caption	Other Details
Combo Box	**CBO_subject**	Caption	
Option Button	**OPT_company**	Caption	Company
Option Button	**OPT_Personal**	Caption	Personal
Command Button	**CMD_insert**	Caption	Insert
Command Button	**CMD_cancel**	Caption	Cancel

CONCLUSION

In conclusion, User Forms and user input are essential components of Visual Basic Scripting (VBS) that allow developers to create interactive and user-friendly applications. By utilizing User Forms, developers can design intuitive interfaces, capture user input, and enhance the overall user experience. Incorporating User Forms and effectively managing user input can greatly improve the functionality and usability of VBS applications.

EXERCISES

1. Create a UserForm called "RegistrationForm" that captures user information for event registration. The form should include the following controls:

    a. Labels: "Name:," "Email:," "Phone:," "Event:," "Payment Method:."

    b. Textboxes where the user will enter their name, email, and phone number.

    c. Combobox containing a list of events for the user to select.

    d. Option buttons for the user to choose their preferred payment method (e.g., "Credit Card," "PayPal," "Cash").

    e. Command buttons: "Submit" and "Clear."

Your task is to design the UserForm with the appropriate controls, set their properties, and handle events for the Submit and Clear buttons.

CHAPTER 23

Advanced VBA Techniques and Best Practices

INTRODUCTION

In this chapter, we delve into advanced VBA techniques and best practices to enhance the functionality and efficiency of Excel applications. We explore topics such as initializing control values, working with option buttons, creating custom buttons and user forms, utilizing Add-ins, implementing a case conversion Add-In, and creating menus through code. By mastering these advanced techniques, readers will gain a deeper understanding of VBA programming and be able to build more powerful and user-friendly Excel applications.

STRUCTURE

In this chapter, we will go over the following topics:

- Code to set initial values for the control
- Code for option buttons
- Code for Insert Button
- Code to show a User Form
- Add-ins
- Code for the Change Case Form
- Creating a menu with code

OBJECTIVES

By the end of this chapter, the reader will learn about advanced VBA techniques and best practices to enhance their Excel applications.

CODE TO SET INITIAL VALUES FOR THE CONTROL

To set initial values for the control, follow these steps:

1. Select View code from Project explorer.

2. Select the UserForm object.

3. Select Initialize event.

Refer to *Figure 23.1.*

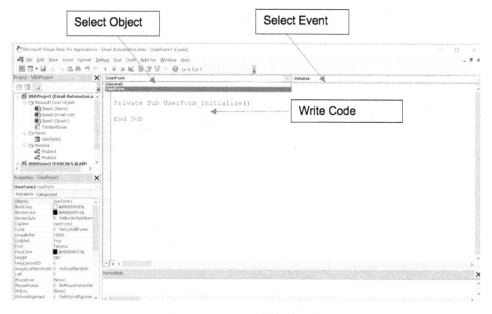

FIGURE 23.1 Setting Initial Values for the Control

The code is as follows:

Private Sub UserForm_Initialize()

```
TXT_name.Value = ""
TXT_address.Value = ""
TXT_contact_no.Value = ""
TXT_company_name.Value = ""
CBO_subject.AddItem "MS Excel"
CBO_subject.AddItem "VBA with Excel"
CBO_subject.AddItem "MS Word"
CBO_subject.AddItem "MS Powerpoint"
CBO_subject.AddItem "MS Office"
CBO_subject.AddItem "MS Access"
CBO_subject.AddItem "MS Project" OPT_company.Value = True
```

End Sub

CODE FOR OPTION BUTTONS

To apply option buttons, follow these steps:

1. Double-click OPT_company

   Private Sub OPT_company_Click()

   When the user selects this option, txt_companyname text box will be visible.

   TXT_companyname.Visible = True

End Sub

2. Double click OPT_personal

   Private Sub OPT_personal_Click()

   When the user selects this option, txt_companyname text box will not be visible.

   TXT_companyname.Visible = False

End Sub

Refer to the following *Figure 23.2*.

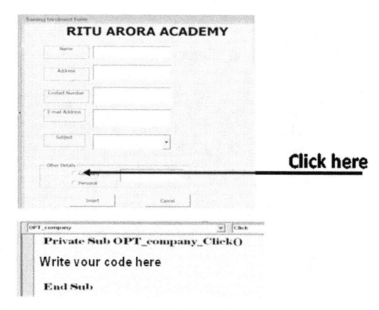

FIGURE 23.2 Adding Option Buttons

CODE FOR INSERT BUTTON

Refer to the following *Figure 23.3.*

FIGURE 23.3 Adding the Insert Button

Double-click Insert Button

```vba
Private Sub CMD_insert_Click()
' Code to find out next blank cell
ActiveWorkbook.Sheets("Training Enrollment").Activate
Range("a1").Select
Do
    If IsEmpty(ActiveCell) = False Then
    ActiveCell.Offset(1, 0).Select
    End If
Loop Until IsEmpty(ActiveCell) = True


' Code to put values from Form to Excel
ActiveCell.Value = TXT_name.Value
    ActiveCell.Offset(0, 1).Value = TXT_address.Value ActiveCell.
    Offset(0, 2).Value = TXT_contactno.Value ActiveCell.Offset(0,
    3).Value = TXT_email.Value ActiveCell.Offset(0, 4).Value =
    CBO_subject.Value If OPT_personal.

    Value = True Then

    ActiveCell.Offset(0, 5).Value = "Personal" Else
    ActiveCell.Offset(0, 5).Value = TXT_companyname.Value


End If
    TXT_name.Value = ""
    TXT_address.Value = ""
    TXT_contact_no.Value = ""
    TXT_email.Value = ""

    TXT_companyname.Value = "Enter your Company name "
    TXT_companyname.Visible = False CBO_subject.Value = ""
    OPT_company.Value = True
End Sub
```

To clear the form after inserting the values, follow these steps:

1. Double-click the Cancel Button.

2. Write the following code:

```
Private Sub CMD_cancel_Click() Unload me

End Sub
```

CODE TO SHOW USER FORM

To run the UserForm from Excel, insert a module and write a macro:

```
Sub Enrol_form()
USR_enrol.Show
End Sub
```

ADD-INS

Add-ins are separate utilities. They provide some extra functionality to the software. The extension name of an Add In is .XLAM. In Excel, we have ready-made Add-Ins, such as Solver, Analysis Toolpack, Conditional Sum Wizard, and so on.

Scenario 31

Create an Add-in to convert the case into upper, lower, or proper, according to the option selected by the user.

Solution

Follow the steps below.

1. Design a form for Add-ins, as shown in *Figure 23.4*.

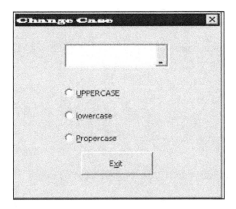

FIGURE 23.4 Designing a Form for Add-ins

2. Open a new Excel workbook.

3. Open Visual Basic Editor.

4. Insert a User Form and name it "Changecase."

5. Assign the caption "Change Case."

6. Drag Objects over the form.

7. Design it as shown in *Table 23.1*.

TABLE 23.1 Option Button

Object	Name	Property	Value
Reference Edit	**Refselect**		
Option Button	**Optupper**	Caption	UPPERCASE
Option Button	**Optlower**	Caption	lowercase
Option Button	**Optproper**	Caption	Proper Case
Command Button	**Cmdexit**	Caption	EXIT

8. Open the code window for the Changecase form.

9. Write code for the different controls.

CODE FOR THE CHANGE CASE FORM

Double-click OPTupper control.

```
Private Sub OPTupper_Click()

    'When user select this option it will convert into
    Uppercase
Dim rng As Range, wscell As Range
Set rng = Range(refselect)


For Each wscell In rng


   wscell.Value = UCase(wscell.Value)
Next
End Sub
```

Refer to *Figure 23.5*.

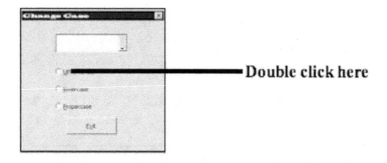

Double click here

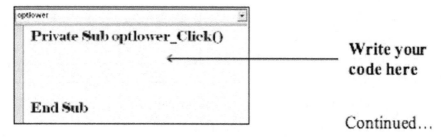

Write your
code here

Continued…

FIGURE 23.5 Lowercase

Now, double-click the OPTlower control.

```
Private Sub optlower_Click()

    'When user select this option it will convert into
    Uppercase
Dim rng As Range, wscell As Range
Set rng = Range(refselect)


For Each wscell In rng


    wscell.Value = LCase(wscell.Value)
Next
End Sub
```

Refer to *Figure 23.6*.

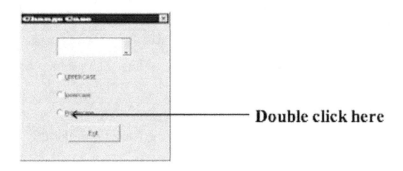

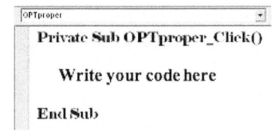

FIGURE 23.6 Proper Case

Continued...

Double-click opt_upper control and write the following code:

```
Private Sub optproper_Click()

    'When user select this option it will convert into
    Uppercase
    Dim rng As Range, wscell As Range
    Set rng = Range(refselect)


    For Each wscell In rng


        wscell.Value = Application.WorksheetFunction.Proper(wscell.
        Value)


Next
End Sub
```

Double-click cmdexit control.

```
Private Sub cmdExit_Click()
End
End Sub
```

Insert a module and write a macro to show the Changecase form.

```
Sub show()
Changecase.show
End Sub
```

CREATING MENU WITH CODE

Refer to the following code:

Sub auto_open()

```
'This code will create a new menu in the existing menubar,
whichwill have one menuitem i.e., Changecase Add-Ins
   Dim newmenu As CommandBarPopup
   Dim menuitem As CommandBarButton

   Set newmenu = CommandBars(1).Controls.
   Add(Type:=msoControlPopup, before:=CommandBars(1).
   Controls("help").Index)
   newmenu.Caption = "E&xtras"


'When Changecase menuitem is selected it should show
changecase form Set menuitem = newmenu.Controls.
Add(Type:=msoControlButton)menuitem.Caption = "&Change
Case" menuitem.OnAction = "show"
```

End Sub

Sub auto_close()

```
'This will remove menu when add ins is removed from the
excelCommandBars(1).Controls("extras").Delete
```

End Sub

In this example:

- *Auto_Open()*: This is the first event that is fired whenever a Workbook is opened.
- *Auto_Close()*: This is the last event that is fired whenever a Workbook is opened.

CONCLUSION

In this chapter, we have explored advanced VBA techniques and best practices that can significantly improve the functionality and user experience of Excel applications. From initializing control values to handling option buttons, creating custom buttons and user forms, utilizing Add-ins, and creating menus through code, we have covered a wide range of topics. By applying these techniques and following the best practices outlined, readers can create more robust, efficient, and user-friendly Excel applications. With a solid grasp of these advanced techniques, readers will be well-equipped to take their VBA skills to the next level.

EXERCISES

Let us consider an example-based exercise that combines several of the advanced VBA techniques discussed in this chapter.

Scenario: You are working on a project management tool in Excel. The tool allows users to input project details, track progress, and generate reports. Your task is to enhance the tool by implementing the following features:

1. Add a UserForm called "TaskForm" that allows users to input task details, including task name, assigned person, start date, end date, and status (e.g., "Not Started," "In Progress," "Completed").

2. Implement validation checks in the TaskForm to ensure that all required fields are filled and that the end date is not earlier than the start date. Display appropriate error messages if any validation fails.

3. Create a custom Insert button on the TaskForm that adds the entered task details to a designated worksheet, such as "ProjectTasks." Ensure that each new task is inserted on a new row, then clear the input fields after successful insertion.

4. Implement a menu system using VBA code. Create a new menu item called "Project Management" in the Excel menu bar. Under the "Project Management" menu, add options to open the TaskForm, display a list of all tasks, and generate a summary report.

5. Develop a summary report function that calculates and displays the total number of tasks, the number of tasks in each status category, and the percentage of completed tasks. The summary report should be displayed in a new worksheet named "TaskSummary."

6. Implement an Add-In called "TaskUtilities" that provides additional functions for task management, such as sorting tasks by name or date, filtering tasks by status, and generating specialized reports. Test the Add-In by using it in different workbooks to verify its functionality.

7. Apply best practices for code organization, error handling, and optimization throughout the project to ensure clean and efficient VBA code.

CHAPTER 24

BUILDING CUSTOM ADD-INS WITH VBA

INTRODUCTION

In this chapter, we will explore the process of building custom Add-ins with Visual Basic for Applications (VBA) in Excel. Add-ins are additional functionalities or tools that can be integrated into Excel to enhance its capabilities and streamline workflows. We will cover topics such as protecting Add-ins with a password and using Add-ins effectively.

STRUCTURE

In this chapter, we will go over the following topics:

- Protecting your Add-ins with a password
- Using Add-ins

OBJECTIVES

By the end of this chapter, the reader will learn how to protect their Add-ins with a password, as well as how to utilize Add-ins efficiently to enhance functionality.

PROTECTING YOUR ADD-INS WITH A PASSWORD

To protect your Add-ins with a password, follow these steps:

1. Collapse all the objects of the project (the Excel file in which you have inserted forms and modules for Add-ins).

2. Right-click over that project.

3. Select VBA project properties.

4. Select the Protection tab.

5. Select Lock for viewing.

6. Set a password.

7. Click OK.

   Refer to Figure 24.1.

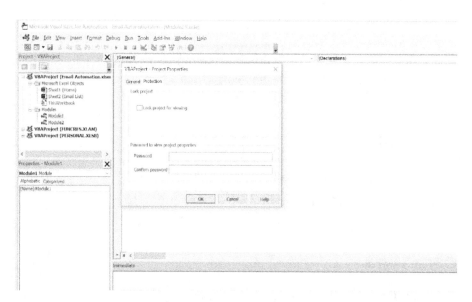

FIGURE 24.1 Adding a Password

8. Once you are ready with the form and modules of your Add-ins, switch to the Excel environment.

9. Save the current file with the type Add-ins (.xlam extension), as shown in *Figure 24.2*.

FIGURE 24.2 Saving the Current File

USING ADD-INS

To use Add-ins, follow these steps:

1. Click on the Office Button.

2. Click on Excel Options.

3. Select Add-ins.

4. Click on the Go… Button, as shown in *Figure 24.3*.

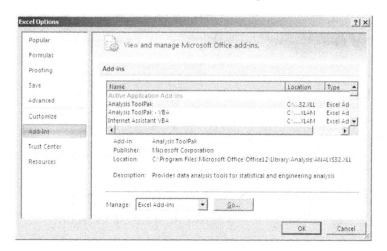

FIGURE 24.3 Selecting the Add-ins

5. Browse to locate your Add-ins, as shown in *Figure 24.4*.

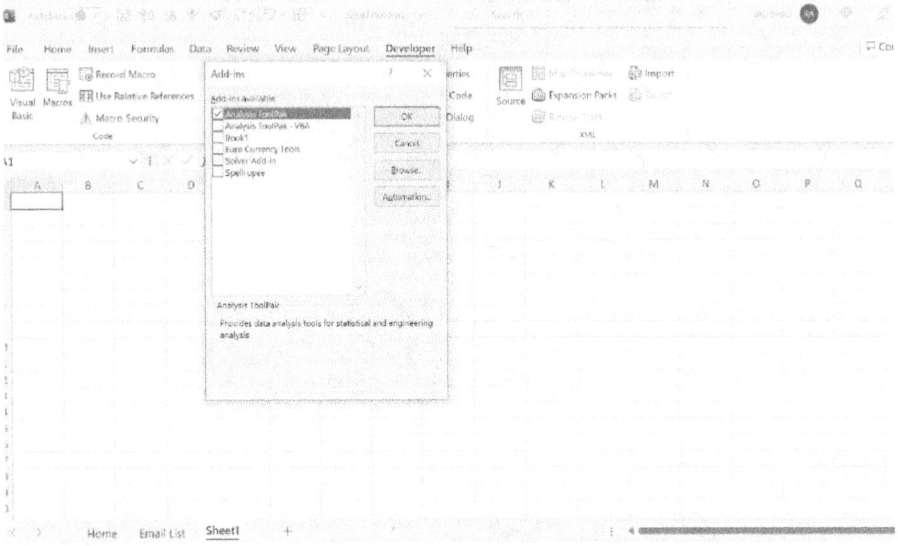

FIGURE 24.4 Locate Your Add-ins

CONCLUSION

In conclusion, building custom Add-ins with VBA empowers users to extend the functionality offered by Excel and streamline their workflows. Protecting Add-ins with a password ensures their security. Utilizing Add-ins effectively enhances productivity and enables users to access additional features and tools within Excel.

EXERCISES

1. Open Microsoft Excel and create a new workbook.

2. Create a simple VBA macro that formats the selected cells with a specific font, font size, and background color.

3. Save the VBA macro as an add-in with an .xlam extension.

4. Protect the Add-in with a password to ensure its security.

5. Test the Add-in by installing it in Excel and using it to format cells in different worksheets.

25

CHATGPT WITH EXCEL

INTRODUCTION

In this chapter, we will explore the integration of ChatGPT with Excel. Excel is a powerful tool for data organization and analysis, while ChatGPT is an AI language model that can assist in various tasks. By combining these tools, you can leverage the capabilities of both to enhance your Excel experience.

STRUCTURE

In this chapter, we will go over the following topics:

- Using ChatGPT with Excel

OBJECTIVES

By the end of this chapter, the reader will learn how to integrate ChatGPT with Excel to further leverage the power of Excel and improve efficiency in tasks such as data analysis, troubleshooting formulas, and formatting.

USING CHATGPT WITH EXCEL

Excel is a powerful tool for organizing and analyzing data. On the other hand, ChatGPT is an AI language model that can provide assistance in various domains, including Excel. Below are some ways you can use Excel and ChatGPT together.

■ Ask for help with Excel functions and formulas. You can ask ChatGPT for help with specific Excel functions or formulas that you are having trouble with. Simply describe the problem or provide an example, and ChatGPT can suggest a solution or provide a step-by-step guide, as shown in *Figure 25.1*.

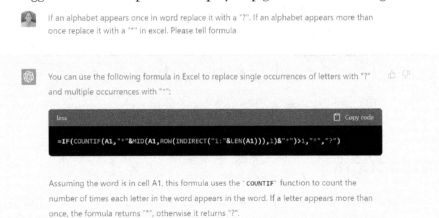

FIGURE 25.1 Asking ChatGPT for Help With Excel Functions and Formulas

■ Get tips and tricks for using Excel. ChatGPT can provide tips and tricks for using Excel more efficiently. For example, you can ask for shortcuts, formatting tricks, or ways to automate tasks in Excel, as shown in *Figure 25.2*.

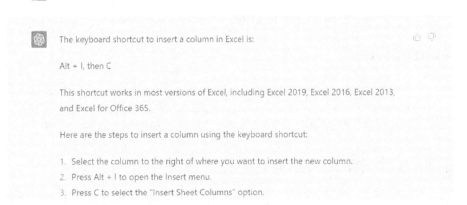

FIGURE 25.2 Asking ChatGPT for Tips and Tricks for Using Excel

■ Get insights from data analysis. Excel can be used to analyze data and generate insights, as shown in *Figure 25.3*. ChatGPT can help you interpret the results of your analysis or suggest new ways to look at your data, as shown in *Figure 25.4*.

CUSTNAME	PRODUCT	PRGRP	QTY	CP	S.P.	NET
Shell Oil	Sony 23" Flat screen	Monitors	6	433.00	585.00	900.00
Anglo American	HP Deskjet Printer	Printers	12	52.00	75.00	900.00
Anglo American	HP M27 Laserjet	Printers	3	275.00	360.00	1,080.00
Anglo American	Compaq H16 250mb	Servers	3	536.00	800.00	2,400.00
Shell Oil	Compaq 1000mb	Servers	2	874.00	1,150.00	2,300.00
Shell Oil	IBM M45 Server	Servers	5	550.00	995.00	4,975.00
Anglo American	Compaq H16 250mb	Servers	4	536.00	800.00	3,200.00
Filofax UK	Sony 23" Flat screen	Monitors	6	433.00	625.00	1,875.00
Rolls Royce	Daewoo M56	Monitors	3	202.00	390.00	1,170.00
Whitbread plc	Sony 23" Flat screen	Monitors	2	433.00	600.00	1,200.00
Filofax UK	Kyocera Deskjet	Printers	4	90.00	120.00	480.00
Rolls Royce	Lexmark G25 printer	Printers	1	110.00	150.00	150.00
Whitbread plc	Kyocera Deskjet	Printers	7	90.00	105.00	735.00
Filofax UK	Compaq H16 250mb	Servers	2	536.00	825.00	1,650.00
P&O Shipping	Eizo 19" CAD	Monitors	5	302.00	450.00	900.00
Rolls Royce	Sony 23" Flat screen	Monitors	4	433.00	650.00	2,600.00
P&O Shipping	Daewoo 23"	Monitors	3	320.00	400.00	1,200.00
Anglo American	Eizo 19" CAD	Monitors	4	302.00	400.00	1,600.00

FIGURE 25.3 Data on Excel

Go to ChatGPT, and in chat, write how to analyze this data. The response is as shown in *Figure 25.4*.

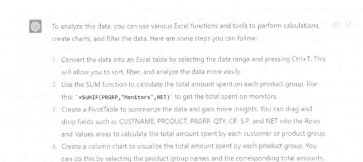

FIGURE 25.4 ChatGPT on How to Analyze This Data

▦ Collaborate on Excel Spreadsheets. You can use ChatGPT to collaborate on Excel spreadsheets with others. For example, you can ask ChatGPT to suggest changes or improvements to a spreadsheet, or to provide feedback on a specific aspect of the data. *Figure 25.5* features a spreadsheet with data.

	A	B	C
1			
2			
3	Row Labels ▼	Sum of QTY	
4	⊟ Anglo American	30	
5	Compaq H16 250mb	7	
6	Eizo 19" CAD	4	
7	HP Deskjet Printer	12	
8	HP M27 Laserjet	7	
9	⊟ Filofax UK	12	
10	Compaq H16 250mb	2	
11	Kyocera Deskjet	4	
12	Sony 23" Flat screen	6	
13	⊟ P&O Shipping	24	
14	Daewoo 23"	3	
15	Dell 260 mb	2	
16	Eizo 19" CAD	15	
17	Kyocera Laser 28ppm	4	
18	⊟ Rolls Royce	15	
19	Daewoo M56	3	
20	Dell 260 mb	5	
21	Lexmark G25 printer	3	
22	Sony 23" Flat screen	4	
23	⊟ Shell Oil	13	
24	Compaq 1000mb	2	
25	IBM M45 Server	5	
26	Sony 23" Flat screen	6	
27	⊟ Whitbread plc	23	
28	Daewoo M56	12	
29	IBM M45 Server	2	
30	Kyocera Deskjet	7	
31	Sony 23" Flat screen	2	
32	**Grand Total**	117	

FIGURE 25.5 Spreadsheet with Data

If you ChatGPT to provide feedback on the pivot table shown in *Figure 25.5,* the following response is generated:

This table shows the sum of the QTY (quantity) of each product sold for each company. To analyze this data, you can:

1. Identify the top selling products - Look for the products with the highest quantity sold. For example, the Sony 23" Flat Screen was the top-selling product with a total quantity sold of 18 (6 + 6 + 4 + 2).

2. Identify the top performing companies - Look for the companies with the highest quantity sold. For example, P&O Shipping sold the highest quantity of products with a total quantity sold of 24.

3. Compare sales between companies - Look for patterns and differences in sales between companies. For example, Anglo American sold a total of 30 products, which is almost three times the number of products sold by IBM M45 Server, which sold only 7 products.

4. Compare sales of products within companies - Look for patterns and differences in sales of products within a company. For example, Filofax UK sold 6 Sony 23" Flat Screens and 2 Compaq H16 250mb Servers, while Shell Oil sold 6 Sony 23" Flat Screens and 2 Compaq 1000mb Servers.

↻ Regenerate response

FIGURE 25.6 ChatGPT Response

■ For Coding in Excel. You can generate any code using ChatGPT, such as a code for converting numbers to words in Excel using VBA.

To convert words to numbers in dollars in Excel using VBA, you can create a custom function that uses the Microsoft Speech Object Library to convert the text to speech and then extract the numbers from the spoken text. Here is an example of how you could do this:

1. Open a new Excel workbook and press *Alt + F11* to open the VBA editor.

2. In the editor, go to Insert | Module, to create a new module.

3. In the new module, copy and paste the code shown in *Figure 25.7.*

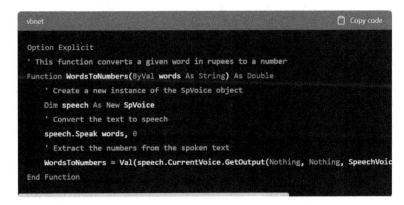

```vbnet
Option Explicit
' This function converts a given word in rupees to a number
Function WordsToNumbers(ByVal words As String) As Double
    ' Create a new instance of the SpVoice object
    Dim speech As New SpVoice
    ' Convert the text to speech
    speech.Speak words, 0
    ' Extract the numbers from the spoken text
    WordsToNumbers = Val(speech.CurrentVoice.GetOutput(Nothing, Nothing, SpeechVoi
End Function
```

FIGURE 25.7 Code to be Copied Into the New Module

4. Save the module and return to your Excel worksheet.

5. In the cell where you want to convert words to numbers in dollars, enter the following formula:

=WordsToNumbers("Two thousand five hundred rupees and fifty paise only")

6. Press *Enter* to calculate the result.

7. This formula will convert the words "Two thousand five hundred rupees and fifty paise only" to the number 2500.50. You can replace the example text with the actual text you want to convert.

The combination of Excel and ChatGPT can help you work more efficiently and effectively with data and can provide new insights and perspectives on your work. Let us say that you have a spreadsheet with sales data for your company. You want to calculate the total sales for each month and create a chart to visualize the data. To do that, you need to follow the steps below.

1. First, you can use Excel to create a new column and use the MONTH function to extract the month from the date in your sales data.

2. Next, you can use the SUMIFS function to calculate the total sales for each month. You will need to specify the criteria for the function to use to sum the sales data for each month.

3. Once you have your totals, you can create a chart to visualize the data. Select your data and go to the Insert tab, then choose the type of chart you want to create.

4. If you are not sure which chart type to use or how to format the chart, you can ask ChatGPT for suggestions. For example, you could ask, "What's the best chart type for visualizing sales data by month?" or "How can I make my chart more visually appealing?"

5. ChatGPT can provide suggestions based on best practices and design principles. You can also ask ChatGPT to explain specific features or settings in Excel if you are not sure how to use them. Refer to *Figure 25.8* for an example.

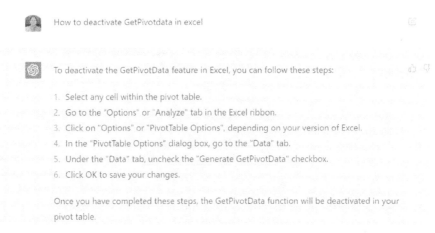

How to deactivate GetPivotdata in excel

To deactivate the GetPivotData feature in Excel, you can follow these steps:

1. Select any cell within the pivot table.
2. Go to the "Options" or "Analyze" tab in the Excel ribbon.
3. Click on "Options" or "PivotTable Options", depending on your version of Excel.
4. In the "PivotTable Options" dialog box, go to the "Data" tab.
5. Under the "Data" tab, uncheck the "Generate GetPivotData" checkbox.
6. Click OK to save your changes.

Once you have completed these steps, the GetPivotData function will be deactivated in your pivot table.

FIGURE 25.8 Asking ChatGPT for Help With Specific Features or Settings in Excel

Using Excel and ChatGPT together can help you work more efficiently and effectively with data and can provide new insights and perspectives on your work.

CONCLUSION

In conclusion, integrating ChatGPT with Excel provides valuable assistance and guidance for users. By leveraging the power of Excel functions and formulas, along with ChatGPT's capabilities, users can improve their efficiency in tasks such as data analysis, troubleshooting formulas, and formatting. ChatGPT can also provide tips, tricks, and insights for using Excel more effectively. Additionally, the ability to collaborate on spreadsheets and seek feedback from ChatGPT enhances the overall experience of working with Excel. By combining these tools, users can optimize their data management and analysis workflows, leading to enhanced productivity and better decision-making.

EXERCISES

1. Open Microsoft Excel and create a new workbook.
2. Enter the following sample sales data in a worksheet.

TABLE 25.1 Sample Sales Data

Dates	Sales
01-01-2023	$500
05-01-2023	$300
10-02-2023	$750
15-02-2023	$600
03-03-2023	$900
07-03-2023	$400

3. Create a VBA macro that performs the following tasks:

   a. Calculate the total sales for each month.

   b. Identify the month with the highest sales.

   c. Display the calculated totals and the month with the highest sales in a message box.

INDEX